Anonymous

Compilation of the Laws of Louisiana Now in Force for the Organization and Support of a System of Public Education

Vol. 1

Anonymous

Compilation of the Laws of Louisiana Now in Force for the Organization and Support of a System of Public Education
Vol. 1

ISBN/EAN: 9783337779498

Printed in Europe, USA, Canada, Australia, Japan

Cover: Foto ©Suzi / pixelio.de

More available books at **www.hansebooks.com**

COMPILATION

OF THE

LAWS OF LOUISIANA,

NOW IN FORCE,

For the Organization and Support of a System of

PUBLIC EDUCATION,

TOGETHER WITH A

DIGEST OF THE POWERS AND DUTIES

OF THE

STATE, DIVISION, DISTRICT, SUB-DISTRICT AND OTHER OFFICERS CHARGED WITH THE EXECUTION OF THOSE LAWS, AND AN APPENDIX FOR GENERAL REFERENCE.

By THOMAS W. CONWAY,
SUPERINTENDENT OF PUBLIC EDUCATION.

'Tis education forms the common mind,
Just as the twig is bent the tree's inclined.—*Pope.*

As this life is a preparation for eternity, so is education a preparation for this life, and that education alone is valuable that answers these great primary objects.—*Bishop Short.*

NEW ORLEANS:
PRINTED AT THE OFFICE OF THE DAILY REPUBLICAN, 57 ST. CHARLES STREET.
1869.

SPECIAL NOTICE.

A copy of this pamphlet is to be furnished to each member of the State Board of Education, each Division Superintendent, each District Board of School Directors, the President or clerk of each Police Jury, to parish Treasurers and State Tax Collectors, District Attorneys, and all other officers and citizens needing information as to the school laws.

Each officer thus supplied should carefully retain the same for reference, among the archives of his office.

The Division Superintendents are especially charged with the distribution of these pamphlets, as herein contemplated, throughout their respective divisions. Such officers and other persons as need copies and are not furnished with the same before the first day of October next, are requested to address their proper Division Superintendent or this office, and they will be promptly supplied.

COMPILER.

OFFICE SUPERINTENDENT PUBLIC EDUCATION,
New Orleans, July 15, 1869.

CONTENTS OF COMPILATION.

CONTENTS OF DIGEST.

CONTENTS OF APPENDIX.

INTRODUCTION.

Special attention of all officers charged with the execution of the provisions of these laws, and all other persons interested in the cause of public education, and all teachers and heads of families generally, is invited to a careful perusal of this compilation, which is the result of a thorough analytical examination of all the statutes of the General Assembly for the establishment and promotion of a general system of Public Education, and of auxiliary acts providing for the systematic training of teachers. All existing provisions of these laws, that are now in operation in the State, have been carefully preserved in the text, and, to avoid confusion and misconception, care has been taken to exclude therefrom all sections, paragraphs and clauses of the statutes that have been modified or repealed by subsequent enactments. The dates and numbers of all acts and parts of acts have been inserted, to facilitate reference to the original statutes, and every effort has been exerted to make this pamphlet complete.

In this compilation appears the "Act to Regulate Public Education in the State of Louisiana, and to raise Revenue for the support of the same" (121 of 1869), and all antecedent acts and parts of acts not repealed thereby; to all of which ready reference can be had by consulting the accompanying Contents.

The annexed Digest has received the greatest care in its preparation, so as to present a complete and convenient conspectus of the powers and duties of the State, division, parish, district, sub-district, and other officers controlled by the provisions of existing school laws, and will, if given frequent and proper inspection, by each officer, of the special duties assigned to him, prove a valuable auxiliary in promoting a more efficient administration of the school system than has ever before been secured to the State; and it is most earnestly enjoined upon all officers to make themselves perfectly familiar with this epitome of their duties; that an unfamiliarity with them may not retard the work of education, and deprive the rising generation of their natural and sacred rights.

In the Appendix will be found title vii. of the Constitution of

1868, relating to Public Education, on which the provisions of Act No. 121, of 1869, are founded; also a brief abstract of such provisions of the laws as relate to the creation, preservation and present condition of the respective School Funds in the State Treasury; a complete text of the law, as now in force, for the government of the State Seminary of Learning and Military Academy, with reference to the act relative to the University of Louisiana; and a memoranda of the amount appropriated by the State since 1866, for the promotion of education.

The "Act (of the United States Congress) to establish a Department of Education," approved March 10, 1867, will also be found in the Appendix, with copy of circular letter issued by the Commissioner of Education, and a "Schedule of information sought respecting Systems, Institutions, and Agencies of Education." The attention of all heads of institutions of learning—public, private, professional, special or class; presidents of colleges and higher institutions of learning, superintendents of asylums for the blind, deaf-mutes, idiotic, juvenile offenders and orphans; superintendents of Sabbath schools; professors and teachers of all private schools, day and evening; keepers of all public libraries, etc., is especially invited to the circular letter and the subject matter contained in the "Schedule of Information," required by the Commissioner.

Division Superintendents will see that a copy of this pamphlet is placed in the hands of all persons above enumerated; and Secretaries of District Boards will make it their especial care to furnish, in their periodical reports as required by law, complete and accurate statements of all such matters as come within their districts. If, in any instance, positive statistics and facts cannot be obtained, estimated reports will be given by the Secretaries, according to their best available means of information.

The cordial aid and co-operation of School Officers, Supervisors, and Teachers of Educational Institutions, and all other good citizens desirous of seeing the State of Louisiana ranked in intellectual advantages, beside any of her sister commonwealths, are earnestly solicited to thus vindicate her honor and dignity.

All necessary information for the promotion of this object not contained in this pamphlet, will be promptly furnished, on receipt of communications, by the Compiler.

THOMAS W. CONWAY,
Superintendent of Public Education.

E. S. Stoddard, Secretary.

AN ACT

To regulate Public Education in the State of Louisiana and to raise Revenue for the support of the same, approved March 10, 1869, *and numbered* 121.

STATE BOARD OF EDUCATION.

SECTION 1. The common schools of the State and such high and Normal schools as may be established and maintained by the State shall be under the management of a State Board of Education, which shall consist of the Superintendent of Public Education and of one member to be appointed from each Congressional District in the State, and two from the State at large in the manner hereinafter provided. Board of Education.

SEC. 2. No person shall be eligible as a member of the said board who shall not have attained the age of thirty years, and shall have been one year a citizen of the State. Who eligible as a member.

SEC. 3. The members of said board shall hold their office for the term of four years and until their successors are appointed and qualified. Term of office.

After the first appointment under this act the board shall be divided as nearly as practicable into two equal classes, and the seats of the first class shall be vacated after the expiration of two years; and one-half of the board shall be appointed every two years thereafter.

SEC. 4. The first session of the Board of Education shall be held at the seat of government, on the first Monday of March next ensuing, or as soon thereafter as practicable, after which the board may fix the time and place of meetings. First session.

SEC. 5. The Superintendent of Public Education shall be *ex officio* President and the executive officer of the board. Superintendent President of Board.

SEC. 6. The board shall have power to make all needful rules and regulations for the government of schools, and for the examination and superintendence of teachers, in pursuance of the laws of the State, on such subjects made and provided, which rules and regulations shall be binding upon all officers of the public schools. Powers.

SEC. 7. The members of the Board of Education, except the State Superintendent of Education, shall each receive a salary of one thousand ($1000) dollars per annum, payable quarterly upon the warrant of the board, approved by the President. Salaries.

Quorum. SEC. 8. A majority of the board shall constitute a quorum for the transaction of business; but no rule or regulation for the government of common schools, or of high or Normal schools shall pass without the concurrence of a majority of all the members of the board, which shall be expressed by the yeas and nays.

Text books. They shall recommend a uniform series of text books for use in all the common schools and the Normal schools of the State.

Withhold payment from teachers not complying with rules. SEC. 9. The State Board of Education shall have power to direct and cause the district director, treasurer, or any other school officer within the State, to withhold from any officer or teacher any part of the public school fund, until such officer or teacher shall have complied with all the provisions of this act, relating to his, her or their duties, and such rules and regulations as the board may prescribe, not inconsistent with the provisions of this act, and the State Board may forbid the payment of any part of the public school fund to any district in which the school or schools have not been kept in accordance to law, or in which no schools have been kept for six months during the year next preceding the demand for payment, and the State Board may direct all public school money thus withheld forfeited; and the amount so forfeited shall be paid into the treasury of the State, to be appropriated for the benefit of the common school fund.

School directors for city of New Orleans and incorporated towns and villages. SEC. 10. The State Board of Education shall appoint for the city of New Orleans a Board of School Directors of nine members, and for each other incorporated city, town or village in the State a Board of School Directors of not less than three (3) nor more than five (5) members, who shall exercise all the powers and duties herein conferred upon district boards of directors, and shall hold their offices for two years, and until their successors shall be duly elected and qualified according to law; *provided*, that in the city of New Orleans the Board of School Directors shall appoint for each ward a board of district directors, who shall have the same powers and discharge the same duties hereinbefore conferred upon boards of district directors in the State, and shall hold their office for two years, and until their successors shall be duly elected and qualified as hereinafter provided.

Appointment of members of State Board. SEC. 11. Immediately upon the passage of this act it shall be the duty of the Governor to nominate and by and with the advice and consent of the Senate, appoint seven members of the State Board of Education, one from each Congressional District in the State, and two from the State at large, who, with the Superintendent of Public Education, shall constitute the State Board of Education created by this act.

STATE SUPERINTENDENT OF PUBLIC EDUCATION.

Sec. 12. An office shall be provided for the State Superintendent of Public Education, at the seat of government, in which he shall file all papers, reports and public documents transmitted to him by the Division Superintendents of the several divisions, each year separately, and hold the same in readiness to be exhibited to the Governor, or to a committee from either house of the General Assembly, or to the State Board of Education, at any time when required, and shall require to be kept a fair record of all matters pertaining to his office. Office of Superintendent.

Sec. 13. The State Superintendent of Public Education shall be charged with the general supervision of all the Division Superintendents, and all the common, high or Normal schools of the State; and he shall see that the school system is, as early as practicable, carried into effect, and put in uniform operation. Duty of Superintendent.

Sec. 14. With a general view to these special duties, he shall meet the Division Superintendents of each Congressional District (School Division) at least once in each year, at such time and place as he may appoint, giving due notice of such meeting; and it is hereby made the duty of the said Division Superintendents to attend each meeting, the object of which shall be to accumulate valuable facts relative to common schools, to compare views, discuss principles, and in general to listen to all communications and suggestions, and enter into all discussions relative to the compensation of teachers, their qualifications, branches taught, method of instruction, text books, division libraries, apparatus, and of all other matters embraced in the common school system. Meetings with division superintendents.

Sec 15. He shall visit such schools as he may have it in his power to do, and witness the manner in which they are conducted. Schools to be visited.

Sec. 16. The Superintendent of Public Education shall cause as many copies of this act, and all other school acts in force, with the forms, regulations and instructions herein contemplated thereto annexed, to be, from time to time printed and distributed among the Division Superintendents as he shall deem expedient, directing the latter to distribute the same among the several school divisions of the State. He shall also prepare, and cause to be distributed to the several division superintendents, a form of certificate in blank, to be granted to teachers; also, all other blank forms necessary to be used in carrying out this act, and all other acts. Distribution of school documents.

Sec. 17. He shall annually, on the first day of January, report to the Auditor of State the number of persons in each parish of the State between the ages of six and twenty-one years. Annual report of school children.

Report to General Assembly.

SEC. 18. He shall make a report to the General Assembly and the State Board of Education, at each session thereof, which shall embrace—

Statement of schools and scholars.

First—A statement of the condition of the common school divisions therein, the number of schools in the State, the number of scholars between six and twenty-one years of age, and also the number in each parish who have attended school the previous year, as returned by the several division superintendents, the number of books in the division libraries, and the value of all apparatus in the schools.

Plans for improvement of school fund.

Second—Such plans as he may have matured for the management and improvement of the common school fund, and for the better and more perfect organization and efficiency of common schools.

Other matters.

Third—All such matters and things relating to his office, and to the common schools, as he shall deem expedient to communicate.

Printed report.

Fourth—He shall cause his report to be printed, and shall present five hundred copies thereof to each body, on or before the second day of their session, for distribution.

Teachers' institute.

SEC. 19. Whenever reasonable assurance shall be given by the Division Superintendent of any division to the Superintendent of Public Education, that a number of not less than thirty teachers desire to assemble for the purpose of holding a teachers' institute in said division, to remain in session for a period of not less than six working days, he shall appoint such time and place for said meeting and such lectures as the said teachers shall suggest, and shall give due notice thereof; and for the purpose of defraying the expenses of said institutes there is hereby appropriated out of any moneys in the State treasury not otherwise appropriated, a sum not exceeding fifty dollars annually, for one such institute in each division held as aforesaid, which the said Superintendent of Public Education shall immediately transmit to the Division Superintendent in whose division the institute shall be held, who shall pay out the same as the institute shall direct, provided, that a like sum shall be contributed by the district.

Superintendent of schools in parish of Orleans and each other general school division.

SEC. 20. On the first Monday of March, eighteen hundred and sixty-nine (1869), or as soon thereafter as practicable, there shall be appointed by the State Board of Education, one person of literary and scientific attainments, and of skill and experience in the art of teaching, to be superintendent of schools in the parish of Orleans, including the city of New Orléans, and one of like qualifications for each of the other general school divisions, to hold office during the pleasure of the State Board of Education, or until their successors have been appointed:

and to perform such duties as are hereinafter provided or the State Board of Education may from time to time direct.

SEC. 21. The State Superintendent of Public Education shall appoint a Secretary, and shall prescribe the duties of the same, not inconsistent with this act. He shall receive for his salary the sum of two thousand ($2000) dollars per annum, payable in monthly installments by the Treasurer of the State, out of the public school funds, on the order of the State Board. He shall take the usual oath of office. Secretary to superintendent.

SCHOOL DISTRICTS—BOARDS OF SCHOOL DIRECTORS.

SEC. 22. Each jury ward or district, that is now or may be hereinafter organized in the parishes of this State is hereby declared a school district for all the purposes of this act. Each district may be divided into sub-districts in the manner hereinafter provided. School districts.

There shall be appointed by the State Board of Education in each school district a board of directors, to be known as the District Board of School Directors, of —— Ward, parish of ——, State of Louisiana. Board of district directors.

Said Board shall consist of three members, one to go out annually, the first board to draw lots for terms, and who shall hold their office for the term of three years, and until their succession shall have been duly qualified. Term of office.

SEC. 23. In each sub-district there shall be taught one or more schools for the instruction of youths between the ages of six and twenty-one years, for at least twenty-four weeks of five school days each in each year, unless the State Board of Education shall be satisfied that there is good and sufficient cause for failure so to do. Schools in each sub-district.

SEC. 24. Scholars residing in one district may attend school in another, in the same or adjoining parish, with the concurrence of the directors of both districts, and, in such case, their proportion of the school money of the district to which they belong shall be paid to the treasurer of the district in which they attend school; and scholars may attend school in any sub-district of the ward in which they reside, with the consent of the District Board. Where scholars may attend.

SEC. 25. The Board of District Directors, of each school district which is now or may hereafter be organized in the State, is hereby made a body corporate by the name of the "Ward District of ———, in the parish of ———, and State of Louisiana," and in that name may hold property, become a party to suits and contracts, and do other corporate acts. Board of district directors bodies corporate.

SEC. 26. The District Board shall hold their regular meetings on the first Saturday after the first Monday in April and October in each year, and may hold such Meetings of district boards.

special and adjourned meetings as occasion may require. They shall organize by electing from their own number a president and treasurer.

Duties of district boards.

SEC. 27. The duties of the District Board of Directors shall be as follows:

Make contracts.

First—To make all contracts, purchases, payments and sales necessary to carry out any vote of the district; *provided*, that before erecting any school house they shall consult with the Superintendent of Public Education, as to the most approved plan for such building.

Admit pupils.

Second—To admit pupils not belonging to the district and not approved of in section twenty-four of this act, to their schools, on such terms as they may agree upon.

Fix number of schools, etc.

Third—To determine the number of schools which shall be established and the length of time each shall be taught, subject to the provisions of section twenty-three of this act.

Fix sites.

Fourth—To fix the site for each school house, taking into consideration the wants and necessities of the people of each portion of the district.

Establish graded schools, and select supervisors.

Fifth—To establish graded or union schools wherever they may be necessary; and they may, as occasion requires, select a person who shall have the general supervision of the schools in their districts, subject to rules and regulations of the board.

Determine branches to be taught.

Sixth—To determine what branches shall be taught in the schools of their district.

Require bonds of officers.

Seventh—To require the secretary and treasurer each to give bond to the district in such penalty, and with such sureties as they may determine upon, conditioned for the faithful performance of their duties under this act. The bond shall be filed with the president of the board, and in case of breach of condition thereof, he shall bring suit thereon in the name of the district.

Examine accounts and report.

Eighth—They shall from time to time examine the accounts of the treasurer, and make settlement with him, and present at each regular meeting of the election a full statement of the receipts and expenditures of the district, and all matters delegated to them to perform, and all such other matters as may be deemed important.

Audit claims.

Ninth—To audit and allow all just claims against the district, and to fix the compensation of the Secretary and Treasurer.

Visit schools, keep lists, etc.

Tenth—To visit the schools in their district, and aid the teachers in establishing and enforcing rules for the government of the schools, and see that they keep a correct list of the pupils, embracing the period of time during which they attend school, the branches taught, and such other matters as may be required by the Division Superintendent.

Eleventh.—They shall, at their first regular meeting after the taking effect of this act, divide their district into sub-districts, such as justice, equity and the interests of the people require; and shall designate said sub-districts plainly upon a plot of the district provided for that purpose, and record the same in the district records; and they may, at any regular meeting, or at any meeting called for that purpose, change the boundaries of sub-districts as circumstances may require, notice of the same having been given at any previous meeting. They shall cause all such changes to be marked on said map or plot, and recorded in the proper book, and in the office of the Parish Judge, and they shall cause new maps to be made from time to time.

Divid district into sub-districts.

Make plot of districts.

Each district board shall adopt a uniform series of books for all the schools in their district, and such series shall not be changed oftener than once in two years.

Adopt uniform series of books.

SEC. 28. A majority of the board shall be a quorum to transact business, but a less number may adjourn from time to time.

Quorum.

DUTIES OF DISTRICT OFFICERS—PRESIDENTS OF DISTRICT BOARDS.

SEC. 29. The president shall preside in all meetings of the board, and of the district; shall draw all drafts on the State Treasurer, for money apportioned to his district, sign all orders on the district treasury, specifying in the order the fund on which they are drawn, and the use for which the money is assigned; and he shall sign all contracts.

President shall draw drafts.

SEC. 30. The president shall appear in behalf of his district, in all suits brought by or against the same, but when he is individually a party, this duty shall be performed by the secretary; and in all cases where suits may be instituted by or against any of the school officers, to enforce any of the provisions herein contained, counsel may be employed by the Board of Directors.

President appear for district in suits.

SECRETARIES OF DISTRICT BOARDS.

SEC. 31. The secretary shall record all the proceedings of the board and district meetings, in separate books kept for that purpose, shall preserve copies of all reports made to the State and Division Superintendents, shall file all papers transmitted to them pertaining to the business of the district, and shall countersign all drafts, warrants and orders drawn by the president.

Secretary shall record proceedings, etc.

SEC. 32. He shall keep an accurate account of all the expenses incurred by the district, and shall present the same to the Board of Directors, to be audited and paid as herein provided.

Account of expenses.

Notice of meetings.

SEC. 33. He shall give ten days' previous notice of all regular and special meetings of the district by posting a written notice in five different conspicuous places therein, one of which shall be at or near the place of meeting of the district board.

File report with division superintendent.

SEC. 34. On or before the twentieth day of September in each year, the secretary of each school district shall file with the Division Superintendent a report of the affairs of the district, which shall contain the following items, viz :

Children in districts.

First—The number of persons, male and female each, in his district, between the ages of six and twenty-one years.

Schools, etc.

Second—The number of schools and the branches taught.

Pupils in attendance.

Third—The number of pupils and the average attendance of the same in the school.

Teachers.

Fourth—The number of teachers employed, and the average compensation paid per week, distinguishing males from females.

Length of school time.

Fifth—The length of school in days, and average cost of tuition per week for each scholar.

Wages of teachers.

Sixth—The aggregate amount paid teachers during the year, and the balance of teachers' fund in the treasury.

Text books used, etc.

Seventh—The text books used, and the number of volumes in the district library, and the value of apparatus belonging to the district.

Number and value of school houses.

Eighth—The number of school houses and their estimated value.

Amount of tax raised.

Ninth—The amount raised within the year by tax for the erection of school houses, the amount for teachers' fund and for other purposes of this act, stating separately the amount for each.

Amount of public fund received, etc.

Tenth—The amount of public fund received from the parish treasury, and, if any, from other sources, stating what, and how much from each, and such other information as he may deem useful.

Penalty for failure to report.

SEC. 35. Should the Secretary fail to file his report as above directed, he shall forfeit the sum of twenty-five dollars, and shall make good all losses resulting from such failure; and suit shall be brought, in both cases, by the district, on his official bond.

TREASURERS OF DISTRICT BOARDS.

Treasurer—duties of.

SEC. 36. The treasurer shall hold all moneys belonging to the district, and pay out the same on the order of the president countersigned by the secretary, and shall keep a correct account of all expenses and receipts in a book provided for the purpose.

SEC. 37. The money collected by district tax for school house purposes, and all contingent expenses, shall be called the "School House Fund," and that received for the support of teachers shall be called the "Teachers' Fund," and the treasurer shall keep with such fund a separate account, and shall pay no order which does not specify the fund on which it is drawn and the specific use to which it is applied. If he have not sufficient funds in his hands to pay in full the warrants drawn on the funds specified, he shall make partial payment thereon, paying as near as may be an equal proportion of each warrant.

"School house fund."

"Teachers' fund."

SEC. 38. He shall receive all money apportioned to the district by the Auditor of Public Accounts, and also all money in the parish treasury collected on the district tax, for his district.

To receive moneys.

SEC. 39. He shall render a statement of the finances of the district, from time to time, as may be required by law, and his book shall always be open for inspection.

To render accounts.

SUB-DISTRICT DIRECTORS.

SEC. 40. It shall be the duty of the director in each sub-district, between the first day of August and the fifteenth day of September of each year, to make and keep on record a list of the names of all heads of families in the sub-district, and the number of children in each family between the ages of six and twenty-one years, distinguishing males from females, and to report the same to the secretary of the ward district on or before the said fifteenth day of September in each year. He shall further report the number of schools in his sub-district, and the branches taught, the number of pupils and average attendance of the same in each school, the number of teachers and the compensation of each, the text-books used, the number of school houses and the estimated value of each.

Directors of sub-districts to keep record of families and children.

SEC. 41. He shall, under such rules and restrictions as the District Board of School Directors may prescribe, negotiate and make in his sub-district all necessary contracts for providing fuel for schools, employing teachers, repairing, building and furnishing school houses, and making all other provisions necessary for the convenience and prosperity of the schools within his sub-districts. All contracts made in conformity with the provisions of this section shall be reported to the District Board of School Directors; and said board in their corporate capacity shall be responsible for the performance thereof on the part of the district.

To make contracts, etc.

SEC. 42. He shall have power to dismiss any pupils from the schools in his district for gross immorality, or

To dismiss pupils and visit schools.

for persistent violation of the regulations of the school, and to readmit them if he deems it proper so to do; and shall visit the schools in his sub-district at least twice during each term of said school.

Contracts with teachers to be in writing, etc.

SEC. 43. All contracts with teachers shall be in writing, specifying the length of time the school is to be taught, in weeks, the compensation per week, or per month of four weeks, and such other matters as may be agreed upon, and shall be signed by the sub-director and teacher, and be approved by and filed with the president before any teacher shall be entitled to a warrant for services.

Director to collect debts and give bond.

SEC. 44. He shall collect all debts due his sub-district and shall apply all funds that may thus come into his hands to the specific purpose for which they were designed; but before entering upon said duties he shall file with the President of the Board of School Directors a bond, such as is required of the secretary and treasurer under this act.

QUALIFICATIONS AND DUTIES OF TEACHERS.

Certificates.

SEC. 45. No person shall be employed to teach a common school which is to receive its distributive share of the school fund, unless he shall have a certificate of qualification signed by the division superintendent of the division in which the school is situated; and no certificate shall be valid more than one year from the date thereof; and any teacher who commences teaching without such certificate shall forfeit all claim to compensation for the time during which he teaches without such certificate.

Records.

Second—The teacher shall keep a correct register of the school, which shall exhibit the sub-district, ward, parish and State in which the school is kept, the day of the week, the month and year; the name and age, and attendance of each scholar, and the branches taught; the register to be after the form supplied by the Board of Education

Register of non-resident children.

Third—When scholars reside in different districts, a register shall be kept for each district.

Copy of register filed.

Fourth—The teacher shall, immediately after the close of his school, file in the office of the secretary of the board and transmit to the State Board of Education a certified copy of the register aforesaid.

OF THE DIVISION SUPERINTENDENTS.

Appointment.

SEC. 46. There shall be six Division Superintendents, one for each Congressional district, appointed by the State Board of Education, for the term of two years, who shall hold their offices until their successors in office shall have been duly appointed and qualified.

Oath of officers.

SEC. 47. Within twenty days after his appointment, each Division Superintendent shall take and subscribe his oath of office. On his failure to do so, or if for any other cause there be a vacancy in said office, the State Board of Education shall appoint, upon the nomination of the State Superintendent, a person to fill such vacancy, who shall qualify in like manner, and who shall hold his office till his successor shall have been appointed and qualified.

Examinations of teachers.

SEC. 48. The Division Superintendent shall examine all persons who shall present themselves at the proper time and place, as to their competency and ability to teach orthography, reading, writing, arithmetic, geography and English grammar, and such other branches as may be required hereafter. In making this examination he may, at his option, call to his aid one or more assistants.

Teachers' certificates.

SEC. 49. If the examination is satisfactory, and if the applicant is shown to be of good moral character, he shall receive a certificate accordingly. The names of all those receiving such certificates, and of all those rejected, shall be entered on a register kept by the Division Superintendent, at the date at which they were given.

Meetings for examinations.

SEC. 50. The Division Superintendent shall, once in each three months, at such place as he may designate in his decision, not to be a less number than one for each two parishes, meet all those who are desirous of passing an examination, and for the transaction of all other business within his jurisdiction, in some suitable room at the seat of justice of the parish, or at any other place, as occasion may require, and shall notify the parish judge of the place of meeting.

Deputies.

SEC. 51. If, for any cause, the Division Superintendent cannot be present at the regular day thus fixed, he shall appoint one or more qualified deputies to make the examination in his stead. He shall afterwards issue certificates to those who receive the recommendation of his deputies as aforesaid.

Revocation of certificates.

SEC. 52. The Division Superintendents may revoke the certificate of any teacher in the parish, for any reasons which would have justified the withholding thereof when the same was given. And the Board of School Directors, upon sufficient cause shown, may dismiss any teacher from any school in the district.

Report.

SEC. 53. On or before the fifth day of October in each year, he shall make a report to the State Board of Education, containing a digest of the reports to him by the secretaries of the district boards, and such other matters as he shall be directed to report by the said secretary, and such as he himself may think pertinent and material, and especially such as will show the condition of the schools under his charge. He shall also suggest such improvements in the system as he may think judicious. He shall also, by the fifth day of October in each year, file with the recorder of the parish an abstract of the number of youths between the ages of six and twenty-one years, residing in each ward and school district within his parish.

Youths between six and twenty-one.

SEC. 54. Should he fail to make either of the reports required in the last section, he shall forfeit to the school fund of his district the sum of fifty dollars, and shall, besides, be liable for all damages caused by such neglect.

Penalty for failure.

SEC. 55. He shall, at all times, conform to the instructions of the State Board of Education as to matters within their jurisdiction. He shall serve as the organ of communication between the State Board of Education and the Superintendent of Public Education and District Board of School Directors. He shall transmit to the District Board of School Directors or teachers all blanks, circulars and other communications which are to them directed, and shall entertain and decide all appeals taken from the decisions of District Boards of School Directors.

Duties.

He shall organize and conduct once in each year, for his own division, at such time as after conference with the Superintendent of Public Education may be designated, a teachers' institute, at some central locality in the division, to which access is convenient, and where the teachers will receive the encouragement of hospitality.

Teachers' institute.

In this work the Superintendent will be aided by a professor from the Normal School, or by some practical teacher appointed by the State Superintendent.

He shall also encourage and assist at teachers' associations, to be convened four times each year, if practicable, on the last Saturday of some month in each quarter, in each parish or in several parishes united, urging the attendance of the teachers of the same, for the purpose of mutual conference and instruction in their duties.

Teachers' association.

He shall also report the number of private schools, academies and colleges in the division; number of pupils, male and female; and all other information, in such form as the State Superintendent may prescribe, so as to present a full view of their educational facilities.

Private schools, etc.

The annual salary of the Division Superintendent shall be ($2000) two thousand dollars per annum. He shall perform such duties and make such reports, in addition to those required in this act, as the State Board of Education may determine; and he shall be paid by the Treasurer of the State, upon warrants drawn by order of the State Board of Education, in accordance with the provisions of this act.

Salary.

SCHOOL DIVISIONS.

SEC. 56. The State shall be divided into six general school divisions, as follows:

The First Division shall embrace the parish of Orleans, including the city of New Orleans. First.

The Second Division shall embrace the parishes of St. Bernard, Plaquemines, Jefferson, St. Charles, St. John Baptist, St. James, Ascension, Assumption, Lafourche and Terrebonne. Second.

The Third Division shall embrace the parishes of Iberville, East Baton Rouge, West Baton Rouge, Pointe Coupee, West Feliciana, East Feliciana, St. Helena, Washington, St. Tammany and Livingston. Third.

The Fourth Division shall embrace the parishes of St. Mary, St. Martin, Lafayette, Vermillion, St. Landry, Calcasieu, Iberia, Avoyelles, Rapides and Catahoula. Fourth.

The Fifth Division shall embrace the parishes of Natchitoches, Sabine, De Soto, Caddo, Bossier, Claiborne, Bienville, Jackson and Winn. Fifth.

The Sixth Division shall embrace the perishes of Concordia, Tensas, Madison, Carroll, Morehouse, Franklin, Union, Ouachita, Caldwell and Richland. Sixth.

DUTIES OF THE AUDITOR OF PUBLIC ACCOUNTS.

SEC. 57. For school purposes, there shall annually be levied by the Auditor of Public Accounts, and collected by the Collector of State taxes in the same manner as other State taxes are levied and collected, two mills on the dollar upon all the taxable property in each parish. Tax levied and collected.

SEC. 58. It shall be the duty of the Auditor of Public Accounts to make a report to the police jury of each parish of the gross amount of the tax thus levied upon their parish, and it shall be the duty of the collector of State taxes for each parish to make monthly returns to the Board of Public Education of the amounts of said tax collected by him, and of the persons and property from which it shall have been collected, and to pay over the same to the State Treasurer; and the Auditor of Public Accounts shall, quarterly, on the first Monday in March, June, September and December, apportion the same among the several school districts of the State, according to the number of children in said districts between the ages of six and twenty-one years, and said amounts so apportioned shall be paid by the State Treasurer to the treasurer of each district board, upon the warrant of the president thereof, countersigned by the secretary. Said district board of school directors shall apportion said sums to the several sub-districts, in the same manner as above provided, and shall from said apportionment pay Tax to be apportioned.

all claims against such sub-districts upon the warrant of the director thereof, approved by the president of the board of district school directors, and countersigned by the secretary.

DISTRICT WARD MEETINGS.

Annual meetings.

SEC. 59. Each ward district shall hold regular meetings annually, on the second Monday in March, at which all the qualified electors of the district may attend; said meetings shall be presided over by the president of the district board of school directors, and the secretary of said board shall be the secretary of the meeting.

Levying of school tax, etc., at ward meetings.

SEC. 60. The electors of a district, when legally assembled at a district school meeting, shall have power to levy such tax, not exceeding three mills on the dollar in any one year, on the taxable property of the district, as the meeting shall deem sufficient to purchase or lease a suitable site for a school house or school houses, and to build, rent, or purchase a school house or school houses, and to keep in repair and furnish the same with the necessary fuel and appendages, and for compensation of teachers, and for procuring district libraries and apparatus for the schools, books and stationery for the board and district meetings, and defray all other contingent expenses of the district; *provided*, that no tax shall be levied for building school houses, excepting at the regular meeting in March; *and provided further*, that no more than five (5) mills on the dollar shall be levied in any one year for school house purposes.

Collector to collect.

SEC. 61. Whenever any tax has been voted, at the regular meeting of the electors of a district, it shall be considered as by said vote levied upon the assessed value of all real and personal property in the district. The secretary of the meeting shall, within ten days thereafter, certify the same to the board of district school directors, who shall certify the number of mills of the tax thus levied to the collector of State taxes for the parish.

Assessment roll.

It shall thereupon be the duty of said collector to enter the same upon a separate assessment roll, which roll he shall, within ten days after he has been certified of the levy of the tax, submit to the district board of school directors, who shall examine and if correct, approve the same. The tax thus levied shall be collected in the same manner, and by the same officer, as State taxes, and shall be paid over quarterly, at such time as the district board of school directors may direct to the treasurer of the district.

GENERAL PROVISIONS.

SEC. 62. A school month shall consist of four weeks of five school days each. School month.

SEC. 63. Any officer whose term of office is prescribed by this act shall continue in office until his successor is appointed and qualified. Officer to hold until successor is qualified.

SEC. 64. Every person appointed to any office pursuant to the provisions of this act, shall before entering upon the discharge of the duties thereof, take an oath to support the Constitution of the United States and of this State, and also the oath of eligibility, and faithfully to discharge the duties of his office according to the best of his abilities. In case such officer has a written appointment or commission, his oath shall be indorsed thereon. In other cases it may be taken orally. In either case it may be sworn to before any officer authorized to administer oaths. Oaths of office and eligibility.

SEC. 65. When any officer is superseded by appointment, he shall immediately deliver to his successor in office all books, papers and moneys belonging to his office, taking a receipt therefor; every such officer who shall refuse to do so, or who shall willfully mutilate or destroy any such books or papers, or any part thereof, shall be liable to a fine of not less than fifty nor more than two hundred and fifty dollars, at the discretion of the court. Delivery of books, etc., to successors.

SEC. 66. All fines and penalties collected from a district officer by virtue of any of the provisions of this act, shall enure to the benefit of that particular district. Those collected from any member of the District Board of School Directors shall belong to the ward, and those collected from parish officers to the parish. In the two former cases suit shall be brought in the name of the District Board of School Directors; in the latter in the name of the parish and by the District Attorney. The amount in each case shall be added to the fund next to be applied by the recipient for the use of common schools. Fines and forfeitures.

SEC. 67. The Board of Education may make all needful rules and regulations to give efficiency to this law; and should any defect be discovered therein while the General Assembly is not in session, which is evidently the result of oversight, and which, in their opinion, is detrimental to the efficiency of the law, they may supply such defect, and any regulations in their discretion not inconsistent with existing laws, until the matter can be acted on by the General Assembly. In such cases they must report the facts and the reasons thereof to the General Assembly at its next meeting. They may also make regulations fixing the powers and duties of any subordinate officer or board when those duties are not sufficiently defined herein, making a like report thereof, as above required. Discretionary powers of State board.

Jurisdiction of school directors.

SEC. 68. Nothing in this act shall be so construed as to give the Ward Board of School Directors jurisdiction over any territory included within the limits of any city or incorporated village, with the territory annexed thereto for school purposes, which has organized separately as a school district under any other provision of this act.

Special meetings to levy tax.

SEC. 69. If adequate provision has not been made at the annual district meeting for school-house purposes, or the payment of debts in any sub-district, the sub-director may, and shall, at the written request of one-fourth of the electors of the sub-district, call a meeting of the electors of the sub-district; said meeting to be held on the second Monday next succeeding the call of the meeting.

Notice of meetings.

SEC. 70. He shall give at least ten days' notice of any meeting so called, by causing said notice to be read in the presence of each school taught in his sub-district, if during term time; or if no school be in operation, then by posting written notices of said meeting in at least three conspicuous public places in his sub-district.

Payment of judgments.

SEC. 71. When a judgment has been obtained against a school district, it shall be the duty of the District Board of School Directors to pay off and satisfy the same from the proper fund by an order on the Treasurer of the district; and it shall be the duty of the district meeting, at the time for voting a tax for the payment of other liabilities of the district, to provide for the payment of such order or orders.

Bible.

SEC. 72. The Bible shall not be excluded from any school or institution in this State, under the control of the board, nor shall any pupil be required to read it, contrary to the wishes of his parent or guardian.

Appeals to superintendent

SEC. 73. Any person aggrieved by any decision or order of the District Board of School Directors, in matter of law or of fact, may, within thirty days after the rendition of such decision, or the making of such order, appeal therefrom to the Superintendent of the proper district.

Affidavit on appeal.

SEC. 74. The basis of the proceeding shall be an affidavit, filed by the party aggrieved with the Division Superintendent within the time allowed for taking the appeal.

Nature of.

SEC. 75. The affidavit shall set forth the errors complained of in a plain and concise manner.

Duty of superintendent on appeal.

SEC. 76. The Division Superintendent shall, within five days after the filing of such affidavit in his office, notify the secretary of the proper district in writing of the taking of such appeal. And the latter shall, within ten days after being thus notified, file in the office of the Division Superintendent a complete transcript of the record and proceedings relating to the decision complained of, which transcript shall be certified to be correct by the secretary.

Notice to parties

SEC. 77. After the filing of the transcript aforesaid in his office, he shall notify in writing all persons adversely interested, of the time and place where the matter of the appeal will be heard by him.

Testimony.

SEC. 78. At the time thus fixed for hearing, he shall hear testimony for either party, and for that purpose may administer oaths if necessary, and he shall make such decision as may be just and equitable, which shall be final, unless appealed from as hereinafter provided.

Appeal to State board.

SEC. 79. An appeal may be taken from the decision of the Division Superintendent to the State Board of Education in the same manner as provided in this act for taking appeals from the decision of the District Board of School Directors to the Division Superintendent as nearly as practicable, except that he shall give thirty days' notice of said appeal to the Division Superintendent, and the like notice shall be given the adverse party. And the decision, when made, shall be final.

Notice.

No judgment for money.

SEC. 80. Nothing in this act shall be so construed as to authorize either the Division Superintendent or the State Board of Education to render a judgment for money; neither shall they be allowed any other compensation than is now allowed by law; *provided*, that all necessary postage must first be paid by the party aggrieved.

Penalty for refusing admission to pupils.

SEC. 81. Any officer, school, municipal, parish or State, or any teacher of any public school who shall refuse to receive into any school any child between the ages of six and twenty-one years, who shall be lawfully entitled to admission into the same, and who shall comply with such rules and regulations as may be presented by the District Board of School Directors and the State Board of Education, shall be deemed guilty of a misdemeanor, and upon conviction thereof, shall be punished by a fine of not less than one hundred nor more than five hundred dollars, and by imprisonment in the parish jail for not less than one month nor more than six months; and all such causes shall have preference before other criminal cases upon the docket of the court before which it shall be brought; and such person so offending shall also be liable to an action for damages by the parent or guardian of the child so refused.

ADDITION.

School house sites.

SEC. 82. Where lands shall be required for the erection of a school house, or for enlarging a school house lot, and the owner thereof shall refuse to sell the same for a reasonable compensation, the District Board of School Directors shall have the power to select and possess such sites embracing space sufficiently extensive to answer the purpose of school house and grounds.

Suit by landholder.

SEC. 83. Should such landholder deem the sum assessed too small, he shall have the right to institute suit before any proper judicial tribunal for his claim, but the title shall pass from him to the school corporation.

No person shall hold any office under the provisions of this act unless he is a qualified voter of the State.

Failure of officers.

SEC. 84. A failure on the part of any district, parish or State officer to perform the duties imposed upon him in this act, and in the manner herein specified, is hereby declared a misdemeanor in office, upon conviction whereof such officer shall be punished by a fine not less than fifty and not exceeding one hundred dollars, and by imprisonment in the parish prison for a term of not less than thirty days, and not exceeding three months. All prosecutions for offenses against this section shall have precedence over all other cases before any justice of the peace, or parish or district court.

State Seminary of Learning.

SEC. 85. Nothing in this act shall be construed to apply to the State Seminary of Louisiana at Alexandria, it being the true intent and meaning of this act to leave that institution to be controlled by laws heretofore enacted concerning it.

Repealing clause.

SEC. 86. All acts and parts of acts in conflict with this act are hereby repealed, so far as they conflict therewith.

Admission of pupils in normal schools.

SEC. 87. In addition to the students admitted from the representative and senatorial districts as herein provided, there may be admitted fifty pupils, possessed of the required qualifications, who desire to qualify themselves as teachers in private schools and academies, who shall pay such sum per session as the State Board of Education may determine and purchase their own text books.

They shall be subject in every respect, except the filing of written declarations in regard to teaching in the public schools, to the rules and regulations of other students.

Model schools.

SEC. 88. The State Superintendent shall prescribe the course of study and supervise the general curriculum in every particular not provided for in this law. He shall make provision for model, primary and grammar schools, under permanent and highly qualified teachers, in which the students of the Normal School shall have opportunity to practice in the art of teaching.

Salaries in model schools.

The salary of the teachers of the model and experimental schools shall be paid from the tuition fees derived from the pupils of said model schools, and those of the Normal School who pay for their tuition; and any balance that may be required shall be paid by the State Board of Education out of the public school fund.

DUTY OF SUPERINTENDENT IN REGARD TO SCHOOL LANDS.

From Section 29 *of Act No.* 321, *of March* 15, 1855.

SEC. 89. (29.) He shall, through the different district attorneys, inquire annually into the condition of the school sections, and institute such proceedings as may be necessary for their recovery when held illegally by individuals, or for the collection of claims originating in the sale of school lands which may be in arrears; and it shall be the duty of the District Attorney to prosecute the suits; provided, the State Superintendent of Public Education shall be authorized to employ other counsel to prosecute these suits, on the refusal or neglect of the District Attorney to attend to the same. The money, when collected, shall be paid into the State treasury, and the interest thereof shall be placed to the credit of the district to which it belongs.

Inquire into condition of school sections.

FREE SCHOOL FUND.

From Sections 31 *to* 36 *of Act No.* 321 *of March* 15, 1855.

SEC. 90. (31.) The proceeds of all lands heretofore granted by the United States to this State for the use or support of schools, except the sixteenth section in the various townships of the States specially reserved by Congress for the use and benefit of the people therein; and of all lands which may hereafter be granted or bequeathed to the State, and not specially granted or bequeathed for any other purpose, which hereafter may be disposed of by the State, and the ten per cent. of the net proceeds of the sales of the public land which have accrued and are to accrue to this State under the act of Congress, entitled "An Act to appropriate the proceeds of the public lands and to grant pre-emption rights," approved September fourth, eighteen hundred and forty-one, and the proceeds of the estates of deceased persons, to which the State has or may become entitled by law, shall be held by the State as a loan, and shall be and remain a perpetual fund, to be called the Free School Fund, on which the State shall pay an annual interest of six per

What constitutes free school fund.

cent.; which interest, together with the interest of the trust fund deposited with this State by the United States, under the act of Congress approved the twenty-third of June, eighteen hundred and thirty-six, with the rents of all the unsold lands, except that of the sixteenth sections, shall be appropriated for the support of public schools in this State; and donations of all kinds which shall be made for the support of schools, and such other means as the Legislature may from time to time set apart for school purposes, shall form a part of the fund, and shall also be a loan on which the State shall pay an interest of six per cent. per annum.

DUTIES OF PARISH TREASURERS AS TO SCHOOL LANDS, ETC.

Sense of inhabitants as to sale of school lands.

SEC. 91. (32). It shall be the duty of the parish treasurers of the several parishes in this State, to have taken the sense of the inhabitants of the township to which may belong any lands heretofore reserved and appropriated by Congress for the use of schools, whether or not the same shall be sold, and the proceeds invested as authorized by an act of Congress approved February the fifteenth, eighteen hundred and forty-three, entitled an act to authorize the Legislatures of the States of Illinois, Arkansas, Louisiana and Tennessee to sell the lands heretofore appropriated for the use of schools in these States.

Manner of holding elections.

Polls shall be opened and held in each township, after advertisement for thirty days at three of the most public places in the township, and at the courthouse door, and the sense of the legal voters therein shall be taken within the usual hours, and in the usual manner of holding elections, which elections shall be held and votes received by a district director of public schools or a justice of the peace; and if a majority of the legal voters be in favor of selling the school land therein, the same may be sold, but not otherwise. The result of all such elections shall be transmitted to the Parish Treasurer, and by him to the State Superintendent.

Re-survey of lines.

SEC. 92. (33). Before making sale of the school lands belonging to the State, it shall be the duty of the Parish

Treasurer, or other persons whose duty it may become, to superintend the sales, to cause a resurvey of such lines as from any cause may have become obliterated or uncertain; and for this purpose he is authorized to employ the parish surveyor, or in his default any competent surveyor, and the lines thus surveyed shall be marked in such manner as to enable those interested to make a thorough examination before sale ; and all advertisements made for the sale of such lands shall contain a full description thereof, according to the original survey and that required by this section. The expenses of making the survey shall be paid by the Auditor of Public Accounts, out of the proceeds of the sale of the lands, on the warrant of the Parish Treasurer.

Manner of conducting sales.

SEC. 93. (34). (As amended and re-enacted by act 267, of 1858). If the majority of votes taken in a township shall give their assent to the sale of the lands aforesaid, the Parish Treasurer shall forthwith notify the Auditor of Public Accounts of the vote thus taken, and upon his order the said lands shall be sold by the Parish Treasurer at public auction, before the courthouse door, or by the sheriff or an auctioneer, to be employed by the treasurer at his expense, to the highest bidder, in quantities of not less than forty acres nor more than one hundred and sixty, after having been previously appraised by three sworn appraisers, selected by the Parish Treasurer and Recorder of the parish, after thirty days advertisement; but in no case at a less sum than the appraised value, payable on a credit of ten years, as follows, to wit: Ten per cent. in cash, and the balance in nine annual installments, the interest to be paid on the whole amount annually, at the rate of eight per cent. per annum. The notes shall be made payable to the Auditor of Public Accounts, secured by special mortgage on the land sold, and personal security, *in solido*, until final payment of principal and interest. In the event of the purchaser neglecting or refusing to pay any of these installments or interest at maturity, the mortgage shall be forthwith closed, and the Parish Treasurer is hereby authorized to advertise and sell the land as before provided for, and further authorized and required to execute all acts of sale on behalf of the State for any such lands sold. to receive the cash payments and notes given for the purchase, which shall be made payable to the State Treasurer, and to place the same in the office of the Auditor of Public Accounts for collection. All cash received, either for principal or interest from said sales, shall be transmitted by him to the State Treasurer, and any moneys thus received into the State Treasury from sales aforesaid, shall bear interest at the rate of six per cent. per annum, and be credited to the township to which the same belongs, according to provisions of the act of Congress. The result of all sales made by the Parish Treasurer shall be forthwith notified by him to the State Superintendent. The Parish Treasurer shall be authorized to receive the whole amount bid for the lands, deducting the eight per cent. interest which the credits would bear.

DUTIES OF DISTRICT DIRECTORS AND PARISH TREASURERS AS TO UNSOLD SCHOOL LANDS.

Lease of school lands.

SEC. 94. (35.) Should a majority of the legal votes be against the sale of the lands, then it shall be the duty of the district directors where the same may be situated, to secure them from injury and waste, and prevent illegal possession or aggression of any kind, and in conjunction with the Parish Treasurer to lease the same, or any part thereof, for a term not exceeding four years, according to the provisions of the second section of the act of Congress aforesaid, and to inform the State Superintendent thereof. Such lease shall only be made after due notice shall have been given by advertisement for at least thirty days, at two or more public places in the township, of the time and place when the land will be offered for lease to the highest bidder. In all cases ample security shall be required not only for the punctual payment of the rent, but for the protection of the land from all and every kind of waste and injury.

DISPOSITION OF PROCEEDS OF LANDS, ETC.

SEC. 95. (36). All moneys that have been or may be hereafter received into the State treasury, and the interest that has or may accrue thereon from the sale of the sixteenth section of school lands or the school land warrants belonging to the various townships in the State, shall be placed to the credit of the township; and should the people of any township desire to receive for the use of the schools therein the annual interest payable by the State on funds deposited to their credit, or the annual proceeds of the loans, the same shall be paid to the treasurer of the parish for the use of the townships or districts, otherwise the interest shall be an accumulating fund to their credit until so called for.

Disposition of proceeds of school lands.

FREE SCHOOL FUND IN STATE TREASURY.

From Sections 9 and 10 of Act No. 182 of March 19, 1857.

SEC. 96. (9). The interest due upon the capital (of the free school fund) and the interest due upon subsequent sales of the sixteenth sections shall be paid to the several boards of school directors of the districts in which the several sixteenth sections lie, on their own orders, approved by the Treasurer of the parish, at any time within two years after the same shall be due. It shall be the duty of the Auditor of Public Accounts, at the end of every fiscal year, to notify the treasurers of all the parishes in the State of the amount of interest coming to the several townships within the limits of the parish, from the interest accrued during the year then terminated, and at the same time to furnish the State Treasurer and Superintendent of Public Schools with a tabular statement of the amount due to each township.

Free school funds in treasury.

SEC. 97. (10). The rents of the sixteenth sections that may hereafter accrue shall not be paid into the State treasury, but shall be paid to the Parish Treasurer, and shall be subject to the order of the school directors of the districts in which the said sixteenth sections are located, and shall be by the said school directors appropriated to the support of their respective public schools.

Rents of sixteenth sections.

Act for Compensation to Parish Treasurer, No. 33, of March 12, 1859.

SEC. 98. The parish treasurers of the several parishes

Compensation to parish treasurers.

shall be entitled to retain, out of the proceeds of the sales of sixteenth sections effected by them, a per centage of two and one-half per centum on the amount of said sales, to be deducted from the cash payment, and the same shall be in full compensation of their services.

Act (for Collection of Notes) No. 217, *March* 17, 1859.

Collection of claims.

SEC. 99. *First*—The Auditor of Public Accounts is hereby authorized and required to place the notes received from the sale of the sixteenth sections now due and those that hereafter fall due, in the hands of an attorney or attorneys for collection.

Second—The attorneys shall be allowed for collecting all such claims five per cent. and no more.

Act (for Relief of Purchasers) No. 83, *of March* 13, 1866.

Annulment of sales by purchasers.

SEC. 100. In all cases of the sale of the school lands known as sixteenth sections heretofore made, where the purchase money has not been paid, the purchaser or purchasers shall have the right to annul the sale upon application to the District Court of the parish where the land is situated; *Provided*, That the judgment of nullity shall be obtained at the cost of the applicant and contradictorily with the District Attorney in conjunction with the school directors in the district in which said land is situated, who shall be made a party defendant in such suit; *provided*, also, that it shall appear upon the hearing that the value of the land has not been impaired by any act of the purchaser; and *provided* further, that nothing in this act shall be so construed as to entitle the said purchaser to repayment of any part of the purchase money already paid.

Act (Exempting Property of Public Schools from Seizure) No. 151, *March* 14, 1855.

Exempt from seizure.

SEC. 101. Property dedicated to the use of and belonging to public schools, or employed by municipal corporations for that purpose, shall be and is hereby exempted from seizure.

LAWS PROVIDING FOR THE FREE EDUCATION OF TEACHERS.

Normal Department in High Schools—Organized in First District of New Orleans, in 1858.

SEC. 102. Act to establish a Normal Department in the Public High Schools in the city of New Orleans, No. 84, approved March 15, 1858, as amended and re-enacted by Act No. 153, March 16, 1859.

First.—The Directors of the public schools in the municipal districts of the city of New Orleans, are hereby authorized to establish in one or more of the Public High Schools under their charge, a distinct class or division, to be known as the Normal School Department, in which those only shall be entered who desire to receive instruction in the art and science of teaching; said department to contain not less than ten and not more than one hundred pupils, who shall remain therein not less than three months nor longer than three years, and who shall previously, by written pledge, have declared their intention of engaging in the occupation of teaching in the State of Louisiana, for at least two years from the time when diplomas shall have been awarded to them as graduates of said department. Normal school department.

Second.—For the support and encouragment of such Normal School Department there shall be appropriated out of the general fund of the State the sum of fifty dollars for each person receiving instruction therein, in accordance with the conditions hereinbefore prescribed, the said sum to be paid quarterly by the State Treasurer upon the warrant of the Treasurer of New Orleans, drawn on and approved by the Auditor of Public Accounts in favor of the Directors in whose municipal districts such departments shall have been organized; *Provided,* That the session of said department shall be held on five days of each week when not interrupted by national or State holidays, or by annual vacations; and that the number of scholars presented as the basis for appropriation shall be in all cases the average attendance of scholars for the previous quarter; *Provided, moreover,* That said directors Appropriation for support of.

shall furnish satisfactory evidence of the actual establishment and successful operation of such department, and that the total sum so appropriated shall not exceed five thousand dollars per annum.

Reports of.

Third.—The said Directors shall exercise exclusive control over such department and the teachers thereof, but it shall be their duty to make a special annual report to the Common Council of the city of New Orleans, and also a similar report to the State Superintendent of Public Education, during the first ten days of the month of January, showing in detail the condition of such department under their charge, the number of pupils admitted and left, the time of their continuance therein, and the actual expense and the money received for the support of the same.

Graduated pupils.

Fourth.—Whenever the number of graduated pupils shall exceed the number of representative districts in New Orleans, the Superintendent of Public Education shall, upon application being made by the different parishes, distribute the excess among the parishes of the State in such proportion as he may deem just and equitable.

Act (Supplementary) constituting State Normal School, No. 155, Approved March 10, 1860.

Normal schools in city of New Orleans for training of female teachers.

SEC. 103.—The Normal School Department organized on the third day of April, 1858, and now in successful operation in the First District of the city of New Orleans, is hereby constituted and designated a State Normal School for the instruction and practical training of female teachers for the free public schools, and other educational institutions of Louisiana.

Said Normal School shall be open to applicants from every portion of the State who shall possess the qualifications of age, moral character, and mental culture prescribed by the Directors thereof, and who shall have declared their intention to adopt teaching as a profession to be exercised within the State of Louisiana for at least two years after they shall have received appropriate certificates or diplomas from said Directors. So soon as the Common Council of the city of New Orleans shall have provided the sum of ten thousand dollars to aid in the erection of a suitable building, the State will contribute a like sum, which is hereby conditionally appropriated to be paid in four equal installments within two years from the date of action of the Common Council, on the warrant of the Treasurer of New Orleans, approved by the Auditor of Public Accounts; and the title to said building and the site thereof, shall be exclusively in the State of Louisiana: *Provided*, That the Normal School therein accommodated, shall be designated and organized in conformity to the provisions of the first and second sections of the act to which this is supplementary; and that the Directors thereof shall provide for the education of forty-eight pupils, to be selected by the Governor, and appointed annually; said pupils being entitled to remain in the school for two years, and to be educated free of charge for tuition, the State not paying the fifty dollars, as provided in the act to which this is supplementary, for any one of the forty-eight pupils so appointed.

The Directors of the State Normal School shall annually furnish the State Superintendent with an abstract of the names, ages, residences, and qualifications of the graduated pupils of said school, and from time to time, with such other information as he may require.

NORMAL DEPARTMENT FOR EDUCATION OF MALE TEACHERS IN STATE SEMINARY OF LEARNING, NEAR ALEXANDRIA, LOUISIANA.

SEC. 104. Act (providing for Beneficiary Cadets) No. 131, March 28, 1867, amendatory of Section 10, of Act 98, of 1860 and of Section 1, of Act 63, of 1866.

Normal department in State Seminary of Learning.

Each parish in the State shall have the right to delegate to the State Seminary of Learning and Military Academy, to remain four years, unless sooner graduated, a number of beneficiary cadets corresponding with the number of representatives to which such parish is entitled in the House of Representatives, according to act approved March 4, 1859, entitled an act to apportion the representation in the Senate and House in the General Assembly of Louisiana, according to the second census, made in 1858, under the eighth and sixteenth articles of the Constitution; that the Police Jury of each parish, and the Board of School Directors of the city of New Orleans, respectively, shall, at a regular meeting, to be held at least twenty days prior to the first Monday of September, elect such a number of beneficiary cadets as said parish or city may be entitled to as aforesaid, of such age and qualifications as may be prescribed by the Board of Supervisors of said seminary, and cause the cadet or cadets so selected to report in person at the seminary on or before the said first Monday of September: *Provided*, That such cadets as are now actually attending the Seminary from any parish, or from the city of New Orleans, shall be included in the number to which said parish or city is entitled; *and provided further*, That in case of any vacancy in the delegation of any parish or of said city, an election to fill the same shall be held at the first meeting of said jury or Board of Directors, after notice shall have been given of said vacancy by the Superintendent of said seminary, and the cadets so elected shall be entitled to admission into the seminary at such time as the board of supervisors shall prescribe; *and provided further*, that the selection of said beneficiary cadets shall be made from among those who have not themselves, or whose parents have not the means of paying their expenses, which facts shall appear by the certificate of the president of said jury or board of directors; and that said beneficiaries whose education is thus provided for shall be required at the close of their term at said institution to pursue the occupation of teaching school within the State for two years thereafter, and shall be required to report such facts to the Superintendent of said institution; that the sum of four hundred dollars be and the same is hereby annually appropriated for two years to maintain and educate each of said beneficiary cadets, payable quarterly, on the thirty-first day of March, the thirtieth day of June, thirtieth day of September, and the thirty-first day of December, to the Treasurer of said institution, upon the warrant of the Governor, and that this act shall take effect from and after its passage.

SPECIAL PROVISIONS FOR THE FREE EDUCATION OF INDIGENT YOUNG MEN.

In Centenary College, Jackson, La.

SEC. 105. Acts No. 116 and 271, approved March 13 and 14, 1855.

It shall be the duty of the Faculty of Centenary College to have at all times in the institution, and to educate gratuitously, ten indigent young men, to be designated by the Governor of the State. Centenary college.

The college shall be subject to visitation by a committee of the Legislature, and whenever the trustees shall fail to perform any duty required of them by the law, or whenever they shall establish a chair of theology or make sectarian dogmas any part of their course of study, then, and in either of the above cases, the bond heretofore given by them to the State shall be due, and the Treasurer shall proceed to collect it, with legal interest from the time of such forfeiture.

The Board of Trustees of said College shall, after the year eighteen hundred and fifty-five, receive from each Congressional District three indigent students, free from charge for tuition, in addition to the number of indigent students now required by law to be educated in said college; said indigent students to be nominated by the Governor of the State, provided that no more than twelve students shall at any one time be domiciliated within the walls of said college under the provisions of this section; each pupil so received shall be entitled to four years tuition, and no indigent student to be admitted in said college before he has arrived at his thirteenth year. Indigent students.

In University of Louisiana, New Orleans.

SEC. 106. Act (relative to University) No. 320, March 15, 1855.

The Faculties of the University may admit, free of charge, such number of indigent young men of the State, of good abilities and correct moral deportment as they may deem expedient. University of Louisian.

FREE PASSAGE OF CHILDREN OVER PUBLIC FERRIES AND ROADS.

Act No. 162, *of October* 17, 1868.

Free passage of children over public ferries and roads.

SEC. 107.—(1) The free right of passage or conveyance over all the public ferries, bridges and roads (except the ferries on the Mississippi river), which are rented out by the State or parish, or over which the State or parish exercise any control, or for which license is paid or toll exacted, is hereby granted to all children on foot attending free public schools, and no tolls or fees shall be demanded or exacted from said children by the keepers or attendants of said ferries, bridges, or roads in their passage to or from school, between the hours of seven o'clock A. M., and nine o'clock A. M., and four o'clock P. M., and six o'clock P. M.; *provided*, that on Sundays and school holidays, no scholar shall have the right to cross such ferries, bridges, or roads, on terms different from those of any ordinary passenger.

Lessees of public ferries.

(2) This act shall have effect from and after the establishment of free public schools throughout the State, and it shall not apply to any lessee of a public ferry, whose contract or lease was made previous to the date of this act.

EDUCATIONAL BUILDINGS EXEMPT FROM TAXATION.

From Section 2 *of Act No.* 114, *approved March* 9, 1869.

Educational buildings exempt from taxation.

SEC. 108. (2) The following property shall be exempt from taxation: * * * * * * * * * * Colleges, school houses, and other buildings for the purpose of education, and their furniture, apparatus and equipments, and the lots thereto appurtenant and used therewith, so long as actually used for that purpose only. * * * * * *

"Oh, woe to those who trample on the mind,
That deathless thing! They know not what they do,
Nor what they deal with. Man, perchance, may bind
The flower his step hath bruised; or light anew
The torch he quenches; or to music wind
Again the lyre-string from his touch that flew;—
But for the soul, oh, tremble, and beware
To lay rude hands upon God's mysteries there!"

DIGEST OF THE POWERS AND DUTIES

OF THE

State, Division, District, Sub-District, and other Officers.

NOTE—The numbers on the left indicate the sections of the compilation.

I.—POWERS AND DUTIES OF STATE OFFICERS.

1.—POWERS AND DUTIES OF THE GOVERNOR.

11. To nominate, and, by and with the advice and consent of the Senate, to appoint seven members of the State Board of Education, one from each Congressional District, and two from the State at large, who, with the Superintendent of Public Education, shall constitute the State Board of Education.

12. To inspect the records of the State Superintendent.

105. To designate indigent young men for gratuitous education in the Centenary College, Jackson, La.

103. To select and appoint annually forty-eight pupils who shall be entitled to two years free education in the State Normal School.

104. To warrant quarterly for the appropriation for the education of beneficiary cadets in the Louisiana State Seminary.

2.—POWERS AND DUTIES OF STATE SUPERINTENDENT.

1. To be a member of the State Board of Education.

5. To be *ex officio* President, and the executive officer of the State Board of Education.

12. To file all papers, reports and public documents in, and keep a fair record of all matters pertaining to his office, each year separately, and hold the same in readiness to be exhibited to the Governor, or to a committee from either House of the General Assembly, or to the State Board of Education.

13. To hold general supervision over all Division Superintendents, and all common, high and Normal schools of the State, and to see that the school system is carried into effect, and put in uniform operation.

14. To meet at least once a year with Division Superintendents, for general conference in all matters pertaining to the advancement of the common school system.

15. To visit such schools as may be in his power, and witness the manner in which they are conducted.

16. To cause to be printed and distributed among the Division Superintendents, copies of all school acts in force, with necessary forms, rules and regulations annexed; also blank certificates, and all other blank forms necessary for carrying out this act, and all other school acts.

17. To report annually to the State Auditor, on the first day of January, the number of persons in each parish of the State between the ages of six and twenty-one years.

18. To report to the General Assembly and State Board of Education, at each session thereof, which shall embrace:

First—A statement of the number and condition of the schools in the State; number of scholars between six and twenty-one years of age; number in each parish who have attended school during the year; the number of books in division libraries and the value of all apparatus in the schools.

Second—Such plans as he may have matured for the management and improvement of the school fund, and the better and more perfect organization and efficiency of the schools.

Third—All matters and things relating to his office, and to common schools, as he shall deem expedient to communicate.

18. To cause his report to be printed, and present five hundred copies thereof to each branch of the General Assembly, on or before the second day of the session.

21. To appoint a Secretary and prescribe the duties of the same, not inconsistent with this act.

19. To appoint, upon reasonable assurance of Division Superintendents that a number of not less than thirty teachers desire it, time and place of meeting of a Teachers' Institute, and such lectures as such teachers may desire, and transmit amount appropriated for said Institute to the Division Superintendent of the division in which it is to be held.

89. To inquire annually into condition of School Sections, and institute proceedings, if necessary, for their recovery, when held illegally, or for collection of claims originating from sale of such lands, and to employ other counsel to prosecute said suits, in case of neglect or refusal of the District Attorney to attend to the same.

3.—POWERS AND DUTIES OF STATE BOARD OF EDUCATION.

6. To make all needful rules and regulations for the government of schools, and for the examination and superintendence of teachers, which rules and regulations shall be binding on all officers of the public schools.

20. To appoint a Division Superintendent for the parish of Orleans, including the city of New Orleans, and one for each other general school divisions.

10. To appoint a Board of School Directors, of nine (9) members, for the city of New Orleans, and for each other incorporated city, town or village in the State, a Board of School Directors of not less than three (3) or more than five (5) members, to hold office for a term of two years.

22. To appoint in each school district a Board of School Directors of three members, to hold office for a term of three (3) years.

55. To prescribe duties of and require reports from Division Superintendents.

8. To recommend a uniform series of text books to be used in all the common and normal schools of the State.

45. To supply form for school register.

9. To cause any school officer to withhold from any officer or teacher, any part of the public school fund, until such officer or teacher shall have complied with the provisions of this act; to forbid the payment of any part of the public school fund to any district inwhich schools have not been kept in accordance with law, and to declare all public school money thus withheld forfeited.

79. To make final decision in all cases of appeal.

47. To fill vacancies occurring in offices of Division Superintendents.

67. To make all rules and regulations necessary to give efficiency to the law; to supply any defect appearing therein, and any regulation not inconsistent with existing laws, until the matter can be acted upon by the General Assembly, and in such cases to report the facts, and the reason thereof, to the General Assembly at its next meeting.

67. To make regulations fixing the powers and duties of any subordinate officer or board, when those duties are not sufficiently defined, making a like report thereof, as is above required.

4.—POWERS AND DUTIES OF STATE AUDITOR.

57. To levy annually a tax for school purposes of two mills on the dollar, upon all taxable property in each parish.

58. To make a report to the police jury of each parish of the gross amount of the tax thus levied upon their parish. To quarterly, on the first Monday in March, June, September and December, apportion the amount of school tax collected among the several school districts of the State, according to the number of children in said districts between the ages of six and twenty-one years.

92. To pay the expenses of making a survey of school lands, out of the proceeds of the sale of said lands, on the warrant of the Parish Treasurer.

93. To order the sale of school lands, upon notification by the Parish Treasurer that the majority of the votes taken in any township are for said sale; and, when sold, to collect payments for the same.

96. To notify the treasurers of all parishes in the State at the end of every fiscal year, of the amount of interest coming to the several townships from interest accrued during the year from free school fund, and at the same time furnish the State Treasurer and Superintendent of Public Education, with a tabular statement of the amount due each township.

99. To place the notes received from sale of sixteenth sections, when due, in the hands of an attorney for collection.

5.—POWERS AND DUTIES OF STATE TREASURER.

58. To pay the apportionments of the school fund made by the State Auditor, to the treasurer of each District Board of School Directors, upon the warrant of the president thereof, countersigned by the secretary.

21. To pay the salary of the Secretary of the State Superintendent of Public Education, monthly, out of the school fund, on the order of the State Board.

90. To apply annually, and to receive from the General Government, the ten per cent. of moneys due, and to become due to this State from sales of public land.

93. To receive the proceeds of the sales of school lands.

6.—POWERS AND DUTIES OF STATE TAX COLLECTORS.

57. To collect the tax levied for school purposes by the State Auditor.

58. To make monthly returns to the Board of Education of the amount of said tax collected by him, and of the persons and property from which it shall have been collected, and to pay over the same to the State Treasurer.

61. To collect the tax levied for school purposes by the electors of a district in the same manner as State taxes are collected, and pay over the same quarterly to the treasurer of the district.

7.—POWERS AND DUTIES OF SECRETARY OF STATE SUPERINTENDENT.

21. To be prescribed by State Superintendent.

II.—POWERS AND DUTIES OF DIVISION OFFICERS.

1.—POWERS AND DUTIES OF DIVISION SUPERINTENDENTS.

55. To conform to instructions of State Board of Education, as to matters within their jurisdiction; to serve as an organ of communication between the State Board of Education and Superintendent, and the District Boards of School Directors; to transmit to District Boards or teachers all blanks, circulars and other communications which are to them directed,

and to entertain and decide all appeals taken from the decisions of District Boards; to organize and conduct, once a year, each in his own division, a teacher's institute at some central locality, to which access is convenient, and where the teachers will receive the encouragement of hospitality; to encourage and assist at teachers' associations, to be convened four times a year if practicable, in each parish, or several parishes united, urging the attendance of the teachers, for the purpose of mutual conference and instruction in their duties: to report the number of private schools, academies and colleges in his division, number of pupils, male and female, and all other information, in such form as the Superintendent may prescribe, so as to present a full view of its educational facilities; and to perform such duties and make such reports, in addition to those required in this act, as the State Board of Education may determine.

47. To meet with the State Superintendent, at such time and place as he may appoint, at least once in each year, for the purpose of accumulating valuable facts relative to common schools, to compare views, discuss principles, listen to all communications and suggestions, and enter into all discussions relative to the compensation of teachers, their qualifications, branches taught, method of instruction, text books, division libraries, apparatus, and all matters embraced in the common school system.

48. To examine all persons, who shall present themselves at the proper time and place, as to their competency and ability to teach orthography, reading, writing, arithmetic, geography, English grammar and such other branches as may be required hereafter; in making which he may, at his option, call to his aid one or more assistants.

49. To grant certificates to those whose examinations are satisfactory, keeping a register of the same, and also of those rejected, showing date when given.

50. To meet once in three months (having designated the place), all those who are desirous of passing an examination, and for the transacting of all other business within his jurisdiction, and notify the parish judge of the place of meeting.

51. To appoint one or more qualified deputies to make examinations for him, in case he cannot be present, and issue certificates to those who receive the recommendation of the deputies aforesaid.

52. To revoke the certificate of any teacher for any reason that would have justified the withholding thereof, at the time given.

53. To make a report to the State Board of Education on the fifth day of October, in each year, containing a digest of the reports to him by the secretaries of the District Boards, and such other matter as he himself may deem pertinent and material, especially such as will show the condition of the schools under his charge; also, suggest such improvements in the system as he may deem judicious.

53. To file by the fifth day of October, in each year, with the recorders of the parishes, an abstract of the number of youths between the ages of six and twenty-one years, residing within each ward and school district in their parishes.

54. To forfeit to the school fund of his district, in case of failure to make either of the reports required in the last section, the sum of fifty dollars, and besides be liable for all damages caused by such neglect.

76. To notify in writing, the secretary, of the proper district of the taking of appeals within five days of the taking thereof, who shall file a complete transcript of the record and procedure relating to the decision complained of in his (Division Superintendent's) office.

77. To notify in writing, all persons adversely interested, of the time and place when the matter of the appeal will be heard by him.

78. To hear all testimony for either party, and for that purpose administer oaths, if necessary, and make such decisions as may be just and equitable, which shall be final unless appeal be taken.

III.—POWERS AND DUTIES OF DISTRICT OFFICERS.

1.—POWERS AND DUTIES OF DISTRICT SCHOOL DIRECTORS IN THE CITY OF NEW ORLEANS, (BOARD OF NINE MEMBERS.)

10. To appoint in each ward a Board of District Directors, who shall have the same powers, and discharge the same duties, herein conferred upon Boards of District Directors in this State, and to hold their office for two years, and until their successors shall be duly elected and qualified.

OF ALL DISTRICT BOARDS.

25. To be a body corporate, and in their name hold property, become a party to suits and contracts, and do other corporate acts.

26. To hold their regular meetings on the first Saturday after the first Monday of April and October, in each year, and hold such other special and adjourned meetings as occasion may require. They shall organize by electing from their own number a president and treasurer.

27. *First*—To make all contracts, purchases, payments and sales necessary to carry out any vote of the district; *Provided*, That before erecting any school house, they shall consult with the Superintendent of Public Education, as to the most approved plan for such building.

Second—To admit pupils not belonging to their district, on such terms as they may agree upon.

Third—To determine the number of schools that shall be established and the length of time each shall be taught.

Fourth—To fix the site for each school house, taking into consideration the wants and necessities of the people in each portion of the district.

Fifth—To establish graded or union schools, and, as occasion requires, select a person who shall have general supervision of the schools in their district.

Sixth—To determine what branches shall be taught in the schools of the district.

Seventh—To require the secretary and treasurer each to give bonds to the district, in such penalty and with such sureties as they may determine upon, conditioned for the faithful performance of their duties under this act.

Eighth—To examine the accounts of the treasurer, and make settlements with him, and present at each regular meeting of the election, a full statement of the receipts and expenditures of the district, and all matters delegated to them to perform, and all such other matter as they may deem important.

Ninth—To audit and allow all just claims against the district, and to fix the compensation of the secretary and treasurer.

Tenth—To visit the schools in their district, and aid the teachers in establishing and enforcing rules for the government of the schools, and see that they keep a correct list of the pupils, the period of time during which they have attended school, the branches taught and such other matter as may be required by the Division Superintendents.

Eleventh—To divide their districts into sub-districts, and to designate said sub-districts plainly upon a plot of the district provided for that purpose, and record the same in the district records. To adopt a uniform series of text books for all the schools of their district, not to be changed oftener than once in two years.

30. To employ counsel in all cases where suits are instituted by or against any of the school officers, to enforce any of the provisions herein contained.

41. To be responsible in their corporate capacity for the payment of all contracts made by sub-district directors, for providing fuel for schools, employing teachers, repairing buildings, and furnishing school houses and making all other provisions necessary for the convenience and prosperity of the schools.

52. To dismiss any teacher from any school in their district, upon sufficient cause shown.

58. To apportion the school fund, apportioned to their district by the State Auditor, among the several sub-districts, according to the number of children in said sub-districts between the ages of six (6) and twenty-one (21) years, and from said apportionments to pay all claims against said sub-districts, upon the warrant of the director thereof, approved by the President of the District Board, countersigned by the Secretary.

68. To hold no jurisdiction whatever over any territory included within the limits of any city or incorporated village, which has organized separately as a school district, under any provision of this act.
71. To pay off and satisfy any judgment obtained against a school district, by an order on the proper fund.
82. To select and possess school house sites, embracing space sufficiently extensive to answer the purpose of school house and grounds, when the owners thereof refuse to sell the same for a reasonable compensation.
91. To hold (when necessary and authorized) elections in townships as to sale of school lands, and forward result to Parish Treasurer.
94. To secure unsold school lands from injury and waste, and prevent illegal possession or aggression, and in conjunction with Parish Treasurer to lease them, and inform the State Superintendent thereof.
96. To draw on Auditor (through Parish Treasurer) for amount of interest due by State to townships for support of schools therein.
97. To appropriate rents of sixteenth sections to the support of public schools in townships in which said sections are located.
100. To act as defendants, under counsel of District Attorney, in suits for relief brought by purchasers of sixteenth sections.
101. To protect from seizure all property belonging to public schools.

2.—POWERS AND DUTIES OF PRESIDENTS OF BOARDS OF DISTRICT DIRECTORS.

27. To bring suits in name of district, on bonds of treasurer and secretary, in case of breach of conditions thereof.
29. To preside in all meetings of the board and of the district; draw all drafts on the State Treasurer, for money apportioned to his district; sign all orders on the district treasury, specifying the fund on which they are to be drawn, and the use for which the money is assigned, and sign all contracts.
30. To appear in behalf of the district in all suits brought by or against the same, unless individually a party thereto.
43. To approve all contracts with teachers.
59. To preside over the regular meetings of the district.

3.—POWERS AND DUTIES OF SECRETARIES OF BOARDS OF DISTRICT DIRECTORS.

27. To give bond to the district, conditioned for the faithful performance of his duties.

30. To appear in behalf of district in cases where the President of the Board is individually a party.

31. To record all proceedings of the board and district meetings, in separate books kept for that purpose; preserve copies of all reports made to Division and State Superintendents; file all papers transmitted to him pertaining to the business of his district, and shall countersign all drafts, warrants and orders drawn by the president.

32. To keep a correct account of all expenses incurred by the district, and present the same to the Board of Directors, to be audited and paid as herein provided.

33. To give ten days notice of all regular and special meetings of the district, by posting written notices in five different conspicuous places therein, one of which shall be at or near the place of meeting of the District Board.

34. To make report to the Division Superintendent, on or before the twentieth of September, of each year, which shall contain the following, viz:

First—The number of persons, male and female each, in the district, between the ages of six and twenty-one years.

Second—The number of schools and branches taught.

Third—The number of pupils and the average attendance of the same in the schools.

Fourth—The number of teachers employed, and the average compensation paid per week, distinguishing males from females.

Fifth—The length of school in days, and the average cost of tuition per week for each scholar.

Sixth—The aggregate amount paid teachers during the year, and the balance of teacher's fund in the treasury.

Seventh—The text books used, and the number of volumes in the district library, and the value of apparatus belonging to the district.

Eighth—The number of school houses, and their estimated value.

Ninth—The amount raised within the year by tax for the erection of of school houses, the amount for teacher's fund, and for other purposes of this act, stating separately the amount for each.

Tenth—The amount of public fund received from the parish treasury, and, if any, from other sources, stating what and how much, and such other information as he may deem necessary.

35. To forfeit the sum of twenty-five dollars (and make good all losses resulting from such failure) in case of failure to file the report as above directed.

58. To countersign all drafts, warrants or orders drawn by the President of the Board of District Directors.

58. To countersign warrants drawn by sub-district directors on the Treasurer of the Board of District Directors, after having first been approved by the President of the District Board.

59. To be secretary of district meetings.

76. To file in the office of the Division Superintendent, in cases of appeal, within ten days after being notified by the Division Superintendent of such appeal, a complete transcript of the record of the proceedings, relating to the decision complained of, and certify to the correctness of the same.

4.—POWERS AND DUTIES OF TREASURERS OF BOARDS OF DISTRICT DIRECTORS.

27. To give bond to the district, conditioned for the faithful performance of his duties under this act.

36. To hold all moneys belonging to the district; to pay out the same on the order of the president, countersigned by the secretary, and to keep a correct account of all expenses and receipts, in a book provided for that purpose.

37. To keep a separate account with the "teachers fund," and "school house fund," and pay no order that does not specify the fund on which it is drawn, and the specific use to which it is applied, and if there are not sufficient funds in hand to pay the warrants drawn, to make partial payments thereon, as nearly as may be an equal proportion of each warrant.

38. To receive all money apportioned to the district by the Auditor
58. of Public Accounts, and also all money in the parish treasury, collected on the district tax (for school purposes) for his district.

39. To render a statement of the finances of his district from time to time, as may be required by law, and his books shall always be open for inspection.

IV.—POWERS AND DUTIES OF SUB-DISTRICT OFFICERS.

1.—POWERS AND DUTIES OF SUB-DISTRICT DIRECTORS.

40. To make, and keep on record, between the first day of August and fifteenth day of September, of each year, a list of the names of all heads of families in his sub-district, and the number of children in each family between the ages of six and twenty-one years, distinguishing males from females, and report the same to the secretary of the district, on or before the fifteenth day of September, of each year. To also report the number of schools, the branches taught, number of pupils, average attendance of same in each, number of teachers and compensation of each, text books used, the number of school houses and the essential value of each.

41. To make all necessary contracts for providing fuel for schools, employing teachers, repairing, building and furnishing school houses, and making all other provisions necessary for the convenience and prosperity of the schools in his sub-district, and to report all contracts made in conformity with the provisions of this section, to the District Board of School Directors.

42. To dismiss any pupils from the schools in his sub-district for gross immorality, or for persistent violation of the regulations of the schools, and to readmit them if he deems proper to do so, and to visit the schools in his sub-district at least twice during each term of said schools.

43. To sign contracts in writing with teachers, specifying the length of time in weeks the school is to be taught, the compensation per week or per month of four weeks, and such other matter as may be agreed upon.

44. To collect all debts due his sub-district, apply all funds that may thus come into his hands, to the special purpose for which they were designed. To file bonds with the President of Board of School Directors before entering upon duties.

69. To call meetings of electors of his sub-district, upon the written request of one-fourth of said electors, to be held on the second Monday next succeeding the call of the meeting.

whenever adequate provisions have not been made at the annual district meeting for school house purposes or the payment of debts.

70. To give at least ten days notice of any meeting so called, by causing said notice to be read in the presence of each school taught in his sub-district, or, if no schools are in operation, by posting written notices of said meeting in at least three conspicuous public places in such sub-district.

V.—POWERS AND DUTIES OF OTHER OFFICERS.

1.—POWERS AND DUTIES OF PARISH TREASURERS.

91. To take (when necessary and authorized) a sense of the inhabitants of townships, holding an election for the purpose, as to the sale of school lands, and transmit result of said election to State Superintendent.

92. To cause re-survey of uncertain lines, before sale, and warrant on the Auditor for payment of expenses thereof.

93. To notify the Auditor of vote in favor of sale of said school land, and on his order to sell the same, execute deeds, send cash and notes to State Treasury, and notify State Superintendent of result.

94. To conjointly with District Directors, rent unsold lands, and inform State Superintendent thereof.

95. To receive, for use of townships or districts, the annual interest payable by State, or moneys from sale of lands or warrants.

96. To approve, after notification from Auditor, drafts of Boards of Directors for interest due townships in their districts.

97. To collect rents of sixteenth sections, and hold the same subject to order of directors.

98. To retain, for services in selling sixteenth sections, two and one-half per cent. of cash proceeds of the same.

2.—DUTIES OF DISTRICT ATTORNEYS.

66. To bring suit in cases of all fines and penalties imposed upon parish officers.

89. To inquire, annually, into the condition of school sections, institute necessary proceedings, prosecute suits and pay amounts recovered into State Treasury.

94. To aid directors, when requested, in ejecting trespassers from school lands, and in protecting them from aggression.

99. To collect (when authorized by Auditor) notes due from sales of sixteenth sections, at a maximum compensation of five per cent.

100. To defend, as counsel of school directors, the interest of the State and township, in suits by purchasers for annulling sales, etc.

101. To aid directors in protecting from seizure property of public schools.

APPENDIX.

I.—SCHOOL FUNDS IN STATE TREASURY.

CURRENT SCHOOL FUND.

This fund was first created by act No. 200, approved March 19, 1857, and now consists :

1. Of the two mill tax, as provided in the fifty-seventh section of the foregoing compilation, and is estimated at a maximum of about $460,000.
2. Of ninety per cent. of the poll tax as provided in the fourth (5th) section of act No. 114, approved March 9, 1869, estimated at $36,000.
3. Of amount accruing from the license of the Louisiana State Lottery Company, article 5, section 1, act No. 25, of 1868, $40,000.

Section 2 of the first act above mentioned requires that the current school fund shall be used for the support of public schools, and that the surplus of receipts over expenditures for any one year, shall be appropriated to the support of such schools during the ensuing year.

The appropriation out of this fund, for 1869, is $250,000.

Sections 57 and 58, of the foregoing compilation, define the Auditor's duties in relation to said fund ; sections 21, 29, 55 and 58, those of the Treasurer.

FREE SCHOOL ACCUMULATING FUND.

The Free School Accumulating Fund was created by act No. 265, approved March 14, 1855, and is derived from.

1. The interest on the vested proceeds of school lands (1211 bonds, representing $1,193,500) annually, $71,610.
2. The interest on bonds belonging to the "Free School Fund," remaining due after payment to townships.
3. The receipts from sales of sixteenth sections.
4. The ten per cent. tax on estates descending to foreign heirs, and and other funds received in trust for free school purposes. (See section 89 of Compilation).

The Auditor and Treasurer are required to invest such funds, with the Governor's sanction, in stocks, bonds of the State, or bonds of the consolidated city of New Orleans, bearing six per cent. interest, and hold said investment sacred for the accumulation of a fund sufficient to produce, by the dividends derived from it, an amount equal to that required annually for the support of free public schools.

Section 2, of act No. 200, of 1857, repeals other provisions of this act, and those of act No. 181, of 1855. As to such investment and the interest thereon, see Act No. 182, of March 19, 1857, ("in relation to certain debts of the State"); sections 1, 2 and 3, in lieu of section 7, repealed; see section 2, of act No. 48, of March 6, 1858; and sections 8, 9, 10, 11, 12 and 13, of act No. 182, of 1857; and finally, act No. 26, of March 12, 1859.

Section 13 and act No. 26 provide that the receipts constituting the "Free School Accumulating Fund" shall not be mingled with any other moneys in the Treasury, and that the Auditor and Treasurer shall annually report to the Governor the amount belonging to said fund, and invest it in any of the bonds receivable by the State, as securities for the circulation of the banks established under the Free Banking Law.

Section 12 makes the Secretary of State and the State Treasurer joint custodians of the Free School Bonds, and the Auditor the collector of the interest coupons thereto attached.

II.—STATE SEMINARY OF LEARNING AND MILITARY ACADEMY.

ESTABLISHED NEAR ALEXANDRIA, LA.

Act for Organization and Government, No. 228, of March 15, 1858—as subsequently amended, and now in force.

SECTION 1. (As re-enacted by section 1, act No. 98, approved March 7, 1860). The "State Seminary of Learning," established near the town of Alexandria, in the parish of Rapides, shall be hereafter designated as "The Louisiana State Seminary of Learning and Military Academy," and shall be under the direction and control of fourteen supervisors, who shall be a body corporate, under the style and title of the "Board of Supervisors of the Louisiana State

Seminary of Learning and Military Academy," with the right, as such, to use a common seal, and who shall be capable in law to receive all donations, subscriptions and bequests in trust for said Seminary and Academy, and to recover all debts which may become the property of said Seminary and Academy, and to sue and be sued in courts of justice; and in general to do all acts for the benefit of the Seminary and Academy which are incident to bodies corporate.

SEC. 2. (As re-enacted by act No. 14, approved February 14, 1867). The Governor of the State shall be *ex officio* President of the Board of Supervisors, and the Chief Justice of the Supreme Court, the Superintendent of Public Education, and the State Engineer shall be *ex officio* members of said Board. The remaining ten members thereof shall be appointed by the Governor, by and with the advice and consent of the Senate, for four years; and they shall continue to exercise the duties of their office until their successors are qualified, and shall be removed by the same power and in the same manner as provided for in their appointment. The Governor shall select ten members as follows: three from the parish of Rapides, two from the parish of Orleans, and five from the remaining parishes; *provided*, that not more than one member shall be selected from any one of the said remaining parishes.

Said Board shall elect one of the members from Rapides as Vice President, to serve in the place and absence of the Governor; the three members from the parish of Rapides shall constitute an Executive Committee, to be convened, by the President or Vice President, for the transaction of such urgent business and important business as, in the opinion of the President or Vice President, cannot be delayed till a meeting of the Board of Supervisors can be convened; and the proceedings of the Executive Committee shall be submitted to the Board of Supervisors for approval or disapproval at the first meeting of the said Board subsequent to the meeting of the Executive Committee. The Board of Supervisors and the Executive Committee shall hold their meetings at any point designated by the President or Vice President of the Board; *provided*, that one meeting shall be held annually at the State Seminary and Military Academy at the time of the commencement exercises of said Academy.

SEC. 3. (Act No. 98, March 7, 1860, as modified by foregoing second section, 1867). The Board of Supervisors shall have stated meetings at such times as the President or Vice President of said

Board shall deem necessary to convene them, a majority of the whole Board constituting a quorum for the transaction of business; but any Supervisor, who shall fail to attend two consecutive meetings, shall be deemed and considered as refusing to act as such, and upon such failure to attend being notified to the Governor, he shall proceed to the appointment of his successor, in the same manner as hereinbefore prescribed; *provided*, that if such failure be occasioned by sickness or temporary absence from the State, the provisions of this section shall not apply thereto; *provided*, however, that any four members of the board, together with the President or Vice President, shall be a sufficient quorum for the transaction of business.

Sec. 4. (Act No. 98, March 7, 1860, amending section 5 of act of 1858). The Board of Supervisors shall have power to engage a superintendent and other professors, and all other officers necessary for conducting the literary, financial and civil concerns and interests of the said Seminary and Academy, and to remove and displace the same at pleasure; to fix and regulate the salaries of the professors and all other officers, tuition fees, and all other charges; to establish rules for the good government and discipline of the students; to prescribe the duties of all officers, servants, and others; to confer diplomas, upon the recommendation of the superintendent and faculty, on students for proficiency in any branch of science or department of learning; and in general to make all rules and regulations which may be deemed necessary for the proper government of the said Seminary and Academy, and for promoting the objects for which it was founded; but nothing in this act shall be construed as obligating the State to pay any debts contracted by the Board of Supervisors, in case they should at any time exceed the appropriations made for the support of said Seminary and Academy.

Sec. 5. (6th of act No. 228, March 15, 1868). The Board of Supervisors shall, at their first meeting elect a secretary, who shall record, attest, and preserve their proceedings, and a treasurer, who shall give bond for the faithful performance of his duties, and in such sum as shall be determined by the Board.

Note.—Sections 7, 8, 9 and 10 of act of 1858, refer to the original board of trustees and the first board of supervisors, exclusively, except as to the following provisions, which are still in force:

Sec. 6. It shall be the duty of the Board of Supervisors, immediately after their organization, to prescribe the course of studies to be pursued at the Seminary, and the number of professors, and to draw up a project of the system of instruction so adopted.

Sec. 7. The Board of Supervisors shall be charged with the preservation and repair of the buildings of the Seminary, and the care of the grounds and appurtenances.

Note.—Sections 3, 11, 12 and 13 of the act of 1858 have been repealed by acts of 1860, '66 and '67.

Sec. 8. (6th of act No. 98, of March 15, 1860). In the course of study pursued at the said Seminary and Academy, the Board of Supervisors shall cause instructions to be given in the military branches of science; the students shall be called cadets, and shall compose a military corps, under the command of the superintendent and such other professors as may be assigned to that branch of instruction. They shall constitute a guard to all public property, arms, or munitions now there or which may hereafter be assembled there; and the superintendent shall receipt for all such property, arms, or munitions, and shall obey all orders relative to their preservation or delivery as he may receive from the Governor of the State.

Sec. 9. (7). The Governor of the State shall cause to be issued to the superintendent a commission as colonel, and to such other professors as may be assigned to command, commissions as majors, captains, or lieutenants, according to the strength of the command; *provided*, that such commissions shall not entitle the holders to any rank in the militia of the State, or to any claim whatever to compensation other than what is attached to their positions as professors.

Note.—See, in this connection, act No. 202, of March 14, 1860, "providing for the establishment of a 'central State arsenal,' in connection with the Seminary," etc., and act No. 15, of February 19, 1867, "requesting the Secretary of War to revoke his order forbidding the usual military exercises at the Seminary, and to permit their resumption, as has been done at similar institutions in other States.

Sec. 10. (8th of act No. 98, of 1860.) The reasonable expenses of the Supervisors, in going to and attending the meetings of the Board, shall be paid by the State; and it shall be the duty of the Board of Supervisors to set forth in their annual report the amount of such expenses.

Note.—The remainder of this section has been repealed.

Sec. 11. (10th of act No. 98, of 1860). *Proviso:* The beneficiary cadets (in the State Seminary) shall be placed on a footing of perfect equality with the paying cadets in said institution; and it shall be the duty of said Board of Supervisors to report to the Legislature the exact costs incurred in supporting a cadet.

NOTE.—The tenth section of the act 98, of 1860, in so far as it provided for beneficiary cadets, was amended by the first section of act No. 63, approved March 7, 1866, and this first section was re-amended and re-enacted by act No. 131, approved March 28, 1867, which said act appears hereinbefore as section 103 of the compilation.

SEC. 12. (Section 2, of act No. 63, of March 7, 1866.) The State Librarian is directed and required to turn over to the superintendent of said institution copies of any books of which there may be duplicates in the library of the State, for the use of the "Louisiana State Seminary and Military Academy," taking therefor the receipt of said superintendent, which shall be filed in the office of the State Librarian as his vouchers for said books, when called upon to produce or turn over the same.

SEC. 13. (Section 2, of act No. 162, of March 28, 1867). No gambling house or drinking saloon, or store for the barter or sale of any kind of merchandise whatever, shall be established within two miles of said institution.

SEC. 14. (Of act No. 228, approved March 18, 1858). The Board of Supervisors shall at all times conform to such laws as the Legislature may, from time to time, enact for their government, and the said Seminary shall in all things and at all times be subject to the control of the Legislature; and the said Board of Supervisors shall make an annual report to the Legislature during the first week of the session, embracing a full account of the disbursements, and a general statement of the condition of said Seminary.

SEMINARY FUND.

(See Article 136, *of Constitution of* 1845; *Article* 138 *of that of* 1852, *and Article* 145, *of that of* 1864.*)*

This fund is vested in the same manner as the "Free School Accumulating Fund," under act No. 182, of March 19, 1857, already referred to. It consists of one hundred and thirty-eight bonds, representing $138,000, bearing six per cent. interest per annum. (See Auditor's Report of January 1, 1869.)

The appropriations for the re-organization and support of the Seminary, in 1866, 1867 and 1869, have been as follows:

Act No. 63, *of March* 7, 1866.

Interest on fund for 1863, 1864 and 1865	$25,800
For repairs and refitting of building, outhouses, etc	5,000
For renewal of library, apparatus, etc., destroyed or lost during war	5,000
For maintenance of 52 beneficiary cadets, at $300	15,600
For salary of secretary, traveling expenses of supervisors, stationery and incidentals	1,000
Total for 1866	$52,400

Act No. 131, *of March* 28, 1867.

For maintenance of 98 beneficiary cadets at $400	$39,200

Act No. 153, *of March* 28, 1867.

For defraying expenses of supervisors	1,000

Act No. 162, *of March* 28, 1867.

For additional repairs to buildings and improvement of grounds	5,000
For enlarging the library and philosophical apparatus	5,000

Act No. 119, *of March* 25, 1867.

Interest on fund for 1862 and 1866	16,380
Total for 1867	$66,580

Act No. 73, *of March* 6, 1869.

For the erection of three professors' houses	$15,000
For repairs to buildings as now erected	5,000
For the erection of additional outhouses	5,000
For purchase of additional philosophical apparatus and library books	5,000
For traveling expenses of board of supervisors for year 1869	1,000

Act No. 139, *of May* 25, 1869.

Interest on fund for 1869	8,220
For expenses of 98 cadets one year, at $40 per month	39,200
Total for 1869	$78,420

Payable to treasurer of Seminary on warrant of the Governor.

III.—UNIVERSITY OF LOUISIANA.

IN NEW ORLEANS.

This University, per act No. 81, of March 3, 1860, is under the control and supervision of eleven administrators, of which body the Governor, Chief Justice of the State and the Mayor of New Orleans are *ex officio* members, the remaining eight being appointed every four years by the Governor, by and with the advice and consent of the Senate. The administrators receive no compensation for their services.

The powers and duties of the administrators are defined in section 2 *et seq.* of act No. 320, approved March 15, 1855. Of the four departments or faculties, of which the University should be composed, according to said act, and the 143d Article of the Constitution of 1864, but two have been organized, viz: those of Law and Medicine. (See Art. 142, of Constitution of 1868).

The appropriations in 1866 and 1867 "for the relief of the University," have been as follows:

Act No. 130, *March* 22, 1866.

For repairs of buildings and to maintain the University.....$25,000

Act No. 182, *of March* 28, 1867.

For fitting up library, lecture and professors' rooms, and completing repairs.. 3,000

Total.......................................$28,000

IV.—INSTITUTIONS OF LEARNING GENERALLY.

Act No. 267, *approved March* 14, 1855.

SECTION 1. The president and trustees of any institution of learning established in the State of Louisiana, which is or may be hereafter incorporated as a body politic, in conformity with the Constitution and laws of the State, who may wish so to do, can deposit in the Treasury of the State of Louisiana, all sums of money intended solely for the uses and purposes of such institutions of learning; and all sums so deposited shall be invested in the bonds or obligations of the State of Louisiana or of the United States, and the interest accruing thereon, as realized, shall be paid over to such corporation, or again invested as they may desire.

SEC. 2. Should any endowment be made, either by donations *inter vivos* or *mortis causa*, to establish a professorship in any institution of learning in the State duly incorporated, on the principal being deposited in the State Treasury, the same shall be invested, and the interest as realized shall be paid over as stipulated in the preceding section; and it shall be the duty of the Auditor of Public Accounts and the State Treasurer to make the investments to the greatest advantage and interest of said institution.

MISCELLANEOUS APPROPRIATIONS, ETC., FOR BENEFIT OF EDUCATION.

Act No. 156, *of March* 22, 1866.

For purchase of 2666 copies of Spencer's English Grammar for gratuitous distribution throughout the State (from Current School Fund) $2,000

Act No. 184, *of March* 28, 1867.

For repairs to Poydras College, parish of Pointe Coupee, (from Current School Fund) $2,500

Act No. 154, *of March* 28, 1867.

Lands belonging to the State laboratory at Mount Lebanon, Bienville parish, donated to trustees for the use and benefit of Mount Lebanon Female College ....

Act No. 163, *of October* 19, 1868.

For Third District Indigent Orphan School, Greatmen street, New Orleans $2,500

V.—CONSTITUTION OF 1868, TITLE VII.

PUBLIC EDUCATION.

ARTICLE 135. The General Assembly shall establish at least one free public school in every parish throughout the State, and shall provide for its support by taxation or otherwise. All children of this

State, between the ages of six (6) and twenty-one (21) years, shall be admitted to the public schools or other institutions of learning sustained or established by the State, in common, without distiction of race, color or previous condition. There shall be no separate schools or institutions of learning established exclusively for any race by the State of Louisiana.

Art. 136. No municipal corporation shall make any rules or regulations contrary to the spirit and intention of article one hundred and thirty-five (135).

Art. 137. There shall be elected by the qualified electors of this State a Superintendent of Public Education, who shall hold his office for four years. His duties shall be prescribed by law, and he shall have the supervision and the general control of all public schools throughout the State. He shall receive a salary of five thousand dollars per annum, payable quarterly, on his own warrant.

Art. 138. The general exercises in the public schools shall be conducted in the English language.

Art. 139. The proceeds of all lands heretofore granted by the United States, for the use and support of public schools, and of all lands or other property which may hereafter be bequeathed for that purpose, and of all lands which may be granted or bequeathed to the State and not granted or bequeathed expressly for any other purpose, which may hereafter be disposed of by the State, and the proceeds of all estates of deceased persons to which the State may be entitled by law, shall be held by the State as a loan, and shall be and remain a perpetual fund, on which the State shall pay an annual interest of six per cent., which interest, with the interest of the trust fund deposited with this State by the United States, under the act of Congress, approved June 23, 1836, and the rent of the unsold lands, shall be appropriated to the support of such schools, and this appropriation shall remain inviolable.

Art. 140. No appropriation shall be made by the General Assembly for the support of any private school or any private institution of learning whatever.

Art. 141. One-half of the funds derived from the poll tax herein provided for shall be appropriated exclusively to the support of the free public schools throughout the State, and the University of New Orleans.

ART. 142. A university shall be established and maintained in the city of New Orleans. It shall be composed of a law, a medical and a collegiate department, each with appropriate faculties The General Assembly shall provide by law for its organization and maintenance ; *Provided*, That all departments of this institution of learning shall be open in common to all students capable of matriculating. No rules or regulations shall be made by the trustees, faculties or other officers of said institution of leaning, nor shall any laws be made by the General Assembly violating the letter or spirit of the article under this title.

ART. 143. Institutions for the support of the insane, the education and support of the blind and the deaf and dumb, shall always be fostered by the State, and be subject to such regulations as may be prescribed by the General Assembly.

VI.—UNITED STATES DEPARTMENT OF EDUCATION.

AN ACT TO ESTABLISH A DEPARTMENT OF EDUCATION, APPROVED MARCH 2, 1867.

SECTION 1. *Be it enacted by the Senate and House of Representatives of the United States of America in Congress assembled,* That there shall be established, at the city of Washington, a department of education, for the purpose of collecting such statistics and facts as shall show the condition and progress of education in the several States and territories, and of diffusing such information respecting the organization and management of schools and school systems and methods of teaching, as shall aid the people of the United States in the establishment and maintenance of efficient school systems ; and otherwise promote the cause of education throughout the country.

SEC. 2. *And be it further enacted,* That there shall be appointed by the President, by and with the advice and consent of the Senate, a commissioner of education, who shall be entrusted with the management of the department herein established, and who shall receive a salary of four thousnd dollars per annum, and who shall have authority to appoint one chief clerk of his department, who shall receive a salary of two thousand dollars per annum, one clerk who shall receive a salary of eighteen hundred dollars per annum, and one clerk who shall receive a salary of sixteen hundred dollars per annum, which said clerks shall be subject to the appointing and removing power of the commissioner of education.

SEC. 3. *And be it further enacted,* That it shall be the duty of the commissioner of education to present annually to Congress a report embodying the results of his investigations and labors, together with a statement of such facts and recommendations as will, in his judgment, subserve the purpose for which this department is established. In the first report made by the commissioner of education under this act, there shall be presented a statement of the several grants of land made by Congress to promote education, and the manner in which the several trusts have been managed; the amount of funds arising therefrom, and the annual proceeds of the same, as far as the same can be determined.

SEC. 4. *And be it further enacted,* That the commissioner of public buildings is hereby authorized and directed to furnish proper offices for the use of the department herein established.

CIRCULAR LETTER BY COMMISSIONER OF EDUCATION.

The undersigned desires to obtain, as early as practicable, accurate but condensed information of the designation, history, and present condition of every institution and agency of education in the United States, and of the name, residence, and special work of every person in the administration, instruction and management of the same. Any response to this circular in reference to any institution, agency, or subject included in the following schedule, addressed to the *Department of Education, Washington, D. C.*, and endorsed "*official,*" is entitled, by direction of the Postmaster General, to be conveyed by mail *free* of postage, and will be thankfully received by

(Signed) HENRY BARNARD,
Commissioner of Education, Washington, D. C.

SCHEDULE OF INFORMATION SOUGHT RESPECTING SYSTEMS, INSTITUTIONS AND AGENCIES OF EDUCATION.

A—General condition (of district, village, city, county, and State.) Territorial extent, municipal organization, population, valuation, receipts and expenditures for all public purposes.

B—System of public instruction.

C—Incorporated institutions, and other schools and agencies of education.

I.—Elementary or Primary Education.

(Public, private and denominational, and for boys and girls.)

II.—Academic or Secondary Education.

(Institutions mainly devoted to studies not taught in the elementary schools, and to preparation for college or special schools.)

III.—Collegiate or Superior Education.

(Institutions entitled by law to grant the degree of bachelor of arts or science.)

IV.—Professional, Special, or Class Education.

(Institutions having special studies and training, such as—1, theology; 2, law; 3, medicine; 4, teaching; 5, agriculture; 6, architecture (design and construction); 7, technology—polytechnic; 8, engineering (civil or mechanical); 9, war (on land or sea); 10, business or trade; 11, navigation; 12, mining and metallurgy; 13, drawing and painting; 14, music; 15, deaf-mutes; 16, blind; 17, idiotic; 18, juvenile offenders; 19, orphans; 20, girls; 21, colored or freedmen; 22, manual or industrial; 23, *not specified above*—such as chemistry and its applications, modern languages, natural history and geology, steam and its applications, pharmacy, veterinary surgery, etc.)

V.—Supplementary Education.

(1, Sunday and mission schools; 2, apprentice schools; 3, evening schools; 4, courses of lectures; 5, lyceums for debates; 6, reading rooms—periodicals; 7, libraries of reference or circulation; 8, gymnasiums, boat and ball clubs, and other athletic exercises; 9, public gardens, parks and concerts; 10, *not specified above.)*

VI.—Societies, Institutes, Museums, Cabinets and Galleries for the Advancement of Education, Science, Literature and the Arts.

VII.—Educational and other Periodicals.

VIII.—School Funds and Educational Benefactions.

IX.—Legislation (State or Municipal) respecting Education.

X.—School Architecture.

XI.—Penal and Charitable Institutions.

XII.—Churches and other Agencies of Religious Instruction.

XIII.—Reports and other Publications on Schools and Education.

XIV.—Memoirs of Teachers and Promoters of Education.

XV.—Examinations (competitive or otherwise) for Admission to National or State Schools, or to Public Service of any kind.

THOMAS W. CONWAY,
Superintendent of Public Education,
State of Louisiana.

E. S. STODDARD, Secretary.

SUPPLEMENT TO COMPILATION.

Act of State Board of Education, adopted September 15, 1869, amendatory to section twenty-two of act No. 121, of March 10, 1869, (section 22 of the Compilation). Proviso to be added to said section.

Provided, That all persons appointed pursuant to the provisions of this section, and of section ten of this act, shall be subject to removal by the State Board of Education for neglect of duty, or other cause by them deemed sufficient.

Act of State Board of Education, adopted September 15, 1869, amendatory to section fifty-eight of act No. 121, of March 10, 1869, (section fifty-eight of the Compilation). To be substituted for said section.

It shall be the duty of the State tax collector of each parish to make quarterly returns to the State Superintendent of Public Education of the amount of said tax collected by him, and to pay over the same to the State Treasurer; and the State Superintendent of Public Education shall, on the first Monday of September in each year, or as soon thereafter as practicable, apportion the same among the several school districts of the State, according to the number of children in said districts between the ages of six and twenty-one years, and shall notify each District Board of the amount apportioned to their district; and said amounts so apportioned shall be paid by the State Treasurer to the treasurer of each parish on the warrant of the State Board of Education, countersigned by its secretary. Until the apportionment above provided for shall be made for the school term of 1869-1870, the State Treasurer shall pay to the treasurer of each parish, upon the customary warrant, such amount in advance of its apportionment as the State Board of Education shall determine. The District Boards of School Directors shall apportion said sums to the several sub-districts in the same manner as above provided, and the parish treasurers shall, from said apportionment, pay all claims for educational purposes accruing under the provisions of the act to which this is amendatory, in any school district, not to exceed the amount to the credit of said district, on the warrant of the Board of Directors thereof, signed by the President of the Board, and countersigned by the secretary; and in sub-districts on the warrant of the director thereof, approved by the President of the Board of School Directors, countersigned by the secretary. The various parish treasurers throughout the State, exclusive of the corporate limits of the city of New Orleans, are hereby appointed custodians of all funds derived from any source for educational purposes, and shall perform the duties assigned by this act to treasurers of district boards.

Act of State Board of Education, adopted September 15, 1869, amendatory to section eighty-eight of act No. 121, of March 10, 1869, (section eighty-eight of the Compilation). To be added to said section.

The salaries of division superintendents shall be payable monthly, and of the members of the State Board of Education quarterly, out of the public school fund, upon the warrant of the State Board of Education, countersigned by its secretary.

OFFICE STATE BOARD OF EDUCATION,
New Orleans, La., September 15, 1869.

The foregoing amendments to the "Act to regulate public education in the State of Louisiana, and to raise revenue for the support of the same," No. 121, of March 10, 1869, were this day adopted by the State Board of Education by the following vote :

Yeas—Messrs. O. A. Guidry, Jules A. Mathieu, V. E. McCarthy, E. W. Pierce, John Turner and J. R. West—6.

Nays—None.

J. R. WEST,
President pro tem. of the Board.

E. S. STODDARD,
Secretary of the Board.

OFFICE SUPERINTENDENT OF PUBLIC EDUCATION,
New Orleans, La., September 16, 1869.

The foregoing amendments to the law contained in this supplement were made by the State Board of Education, by virtue of authority granted said Board by section sixty-seven of act. No. 121, of March 10, 1869, (see section sixty-seven of the Compilation), said amendments having been found necessary for the practical and efficient working of the school law.

THOMAS W. CONWAY,
Superintendent of Public Education, State of Louisiana.

E. S. STODDARD, Secretary.

RULES AND REGULATIONS

FOR THE

GOVERNMENT OF SCHOOLS

AND

Subordinate Boards of School Directors,

BY THE

STATE BOARD OF EDUCATION,

STATE OF LOUISIANA.

SEE SUPPLEMENT TO COMPILATION, PAGE 73.

NEW ORLEANS:
PRINTED AT THE OFFICE OF THE DAILY REPUBLICAN, 57 ST. CHARLES STREET.
1869.

MEMBERS OF THE STATE BOARD OF EDUCATION

FOR THE

State of Louisiana.

THOMAS W. CONWAY, President,
W. JASPER BLACKBURN,
O. A GUIDRY,
JULES A. MATHIEU,
V. E. McCARTHY,
E. W. PIERCE,
JOHN TURNER,
J. R. WEST,
E. S. STODDARD, Secretary.

Office—No. 164 Julia Street, New Orleans.

RULES AND REGULATIONS.

CHAPTER I.—GRADES—BRANCHES OF STUDY.

RULE 1.—The different grades of schools in the State of Louisiana shall be designated as Primary, Grammar, High, and Normal Schools.

RULE 2.—In the Primary Schools there shall be taught the rudiments of reading, writing, spelling and arithmetic. In the Grammar Schools there shall be taught reading, writing, arithmetic, English grammar, geography and history of the United States ; and, where practicable, vocal music and drawing.

RULE 3.—The Primary and Grammar Schools shall contain four grades of departments, known as First and Second Primary, and First and Second Grammar departments ; but in sparsely settled districts of country, the Primary and Grammar Schools may be united at the discretion of the local boards.

RULE 4.—The High Schools shall be for the education of all children who are competent to pursue the branches taught therein.

CHAPTER II.—TERMS AND SCHOOL SESSIONS.

RULE 5.—The scholastic year shall commence on the first Monday in September; and in every school district there shall be kept, for at least twenty-four weeks in each year, at such times as the local board may deem most convenient, a sufficient number of schools for the instruction of all the children who may legally attend public schools therein.

RULE 6.—There shall be daily sessions in all the schools, Saturdays and Sundays excepted. These sessions shall be regulated as to their duration and intermissions by the District Boards, but shall be at least of five hours each day, and not exceed six hours.

CHAPTER III.—EXAMINATIONS.

Rule 7.—A public examination of all the schools shall take place at least once in each year; besides which all the classes in the High and Normal Schools shall be examined, in writing, in each branch of study when it is completed.

CHAPTER IV.—VACATIONS AND HOLIDAYS.

Rule 8.—The schools shall be closed from the twenty-fifth of December to the first of January, inclusive; on all Thanksgiving or fast days authorized by the State or General Government, and on all Saturdays throughout the year, and on such other days as may be directed by the District Boards.

CHAPTER V.—TEACHERS.

Rule 9.—The teachers employed for the scholastic year shall hold their office for the full term, unless sooner discharged by the District Board.

Rule 10.—They are required to be at their respective rooms at least ten minutes before the time for opening each session, and shall, in a daily register to be kept by the principal, record their names and hour and minute of their arrival, and any teacher failing to comply with this rule shall be reported by the principal as tardy.

Rule 11.—They shall open school punctually at the appointed time, devote themselves during school hours exclusively to the instruction of their pupils, maintain good order and strictly adhere to the course of study and the use of the text books prescribed by the District Board.

Rule 12.—It shall be their duty to practice such discipline in their school as would be exercised by a kind and judicious parent in his family, always firm and vigilant, but prudent. They shall endeavor, on all proper occasions, to impress upon the minds of their pupils the principles of morality and virtue, a sacred regard for truth, love to God, love to man, sobriety, industry and frugality. But no teacher shall exercise any sectarian influence in the schools.

Rule. 13.—They shall see that the pupils under their charge distinctly understand and faithfully observe all the rules relating to pupils.

Rule 14.—They shall attend carefully to the ventilation and temperature of their school rooms.

Rule 15.—Any teacher who may be absent from school on account of sickness, or other necessity, must cause immediate notice of such absence to be given to the Directors.

Rule 16.—No teacher shall resign without giving two weeks written notice to the President of the board or sub-director, in default of which, all compensation due for one-half month may be forfeited.

Rule 17.—The salary of teachers shall be deducted *pro rata* for absence, except in cases of sickness of teachers, when half pay shall be allowed ; provided, however, that no deduction shall be made for two days absence during the half quarter, caused by sickness of the teacher or death in the family.

Rule 18.—No teacher shall be employed in the public schools who does not hold a certificate of qualification from the Division Superintendent.

Rule 19.—Teachers shall not hold any position of higher grade than the one corresponding to their certificates from the Division Superintendent.

Rule 20.—Supernumeraries shall be paid full pay for their time of service. Any teacher who expects to be absent from his or her post must send notice to the principal before the opening of the school, that a supernumerary may be sent for, and the place supplied for the day.

Teachers who may be absent from their places without satisfactory cause for three successive days, shall be considered as having resigned.

CHAPTER VI.—PRINCIPAL TEACHERS.

Rule 21.—The principal teachers shall keep a register, in which they shall record the name, age, birth-place, residence and date of admission of each pupil for the first time entered in the public schools, and also the name and occupation of the parent or guardian.

Rule 22.—They shall also make a daily record of the pupils admitted, present, absent or tardy, and at the close of each term they shall file the same in the office of the Secretary of the District Board, and at the close of the school year shall forward two certified copies of said reports to the Division Superintendent, one of which shall be forwarded to the State Board.

Rule 23.—The principal shall have a general supervision of the grounds, buildings, and appurtenances of the school, and shall be held responsible for any want of neatness or cleanliness on the premises ; whenever any repairs are needed, he shall give notice thereof to the President of the District Board.

Rule 24.—Each principal shall examine the classes of the assistants as often as practicable, without neglecting the pupils under his immediate charge.

CHAPTER VII.—CONCERNING DISCIPLINE.

Rule 25.—All teachers are required to maintain strict order and discipline in their schools and class rooms, at all times. Any neglect of this requirement will be considered good cause for dismissal. In maintaining order teachers are hereby authorized to employ any proper means which may be necessary to secure a compliance with their commands to the pupils, and in the use of which they will receive the full countenance and support of the District Board.

Rule 26.—All teachers will be held to a strict accountability as to the manner in which they shall use the authority herein delegated, and upon complaint of severity of punishment, each case shall be adjudged upon its own merits, the teacher being subject to instant dismissal if the board decide it to be demanded by the circumstances.

Rule 27.—Those teachers who are most successful in maintaining the order and discipline of their pupils without the use of corporal punishment, other qualifications being sufficient, shall be awarded by the Board a higher degree of appreciation, and receive the preference over all others in promotions and appointments.

Rule 28.—Principals shall be permitted, without interfer nce on the part of any member of the board or the Superintendent, to arrange the details for the internal government of their schools according to their own method, provided such method is not inconsistent with the general regulations of the schools; such principals, of course, being liable to be judged of as to their qualifications by the results they may produce.

Rule 29.—The principals shall be required, within one week after the commencement of each term, to have the programme of their daily exercises posted in the school room in a conspicuous place, and shall transmit a copy of the same to the President of the District Board, and one to the Division Superintendent.

CHAPTER VIII.--PUPILS—ADMISSION, ATTENDANCE AND ABSENCE.

Rule 30.—Every youth, on making application for admittance to the public schools, shall be required to furnish a printed certificate, signed by the President of the District Board of the district or sub-district in which such youth resides, setting forth that the holder is within the legal age, designating the school at which he shall attend, and in case any youth should desire to attend school in another parish or district, such applicant shall be required to present a certificate from the directors of the district in which he resides.

Rule 31.—Children applying for admission into the public schools are required to furnish all the necessary text books prescribed by the State Board, and stationery used in their classes, in default of which they shall not be received.

Rule 32.—No one having been a pupil in one school shall be admitted into another during the same scholastic year, without presenting to the principal a certificate of honorable discharge from the former school, or a permit from the President of the District Board.

Rule 33.—No pupil shall be allowed to depart from school before the usual time unless sick, or on account of some other pressing emergency, of which the teacher shall be the judge.

Rule 34.—Sickness of the pupil, or in the family, or some urgent necessity, shall be regarded as the only legitimate excuse for absence.

Rule 35.—Pupils who have been absent, or who from any cause have failed to prepare their lessons satisfactorily may be required to recite them after school.

Rule 36.—No pupil shall be allowed to be absent from school during the regular sessions to take music, drawing, dancing, or other lessons.

CHAPTER IX.—DEPORTMENT OF PUPILS.

Rule 37.—The pupils must, on all occasions, be obedient to their teachers and polite in their intercourse with each other. They must be diligent in study, prompt in recitation, and observe propriety of deportment during the recesses, and in coming to and going from school.

Rule 38.—Cleanliness in person and clothing is required of every pupil, and repeated neglect or refusal to comply with this rule shall be sufficient cause of suspension from school.

Rule 39.—Any pupil who shall destroy or injure any property of the public schools shall be required to pay the amount lost thereby, and on failure to do so may be suspended from school.

Rule 40.—Any pupil guilty of disobedience to a teacher, or of gross misconduct, may be suspended by the principal, written notice of which, stating the cause, shall be immediately given to the parent or guardian, and to the District Board.

Rule 41.—Any pupil suspended from school by virtue of any of the above rules, can be restored only on such conditions as the Board of Directors shall determine.

CHAPTER X.—SCHOOL MEMBERSHIP.

Rule 42.—When a teacher has satisfactory evidence that a pupil has left school without the intention of returning, such pupil's name shall forthwith be stricken from the roll ; but any absences recorded against the name of the pupil before the teacher receives this notice, shall be allowed to remain, and in making up the attendance averages, such absences shall be regarded the same as any other absences.

NOTE—It is the custom with most teachers to make up the per cent. of attendance every day. In cases (if there are any) where the record of attendance is not entered till the end of the week, or month, or quarter, it is to be distinctly borne in mind that when one or more absences have been recorded against a pupil before he gives notice of his withdrawal, it is then too late to go back and cancel such absences. The rule requires all absences that occur before the pupil is marked as discharged to remain on the records.

RULE 43.—When a pupil is suspended from school by any of the rules of the School Board, whether for absence or for any other cause, his name shall be stricken from the roll.

RULE 44.—When a pupil is absent from school more than five consecutive school days, for sickness or for any other cause, except in case of suspension, his name shall be stricken from the roll at the end of the five days, and the absences shall in all cases be recorded while the name remains on the roll.

NOTE—The design of this rule is simply to fix a limit beyond which the absences of a pupil shall cease to be recorded. It is not intended to put the pupil or his parents to any extra trouble, nor to exclude the pupil from school for a single half-day. Unless suspended by some other rule, he can be received back to the school whenever he returns, just as if no such rule as this existed. By dropping the name from the roll at the end of five days the absences cease to be recorded till the pupil re-enters.

CHAPTER XI.—SCHOOL DIRECTORS.

RULE 45.—If for any cause it is found necessary to dismiss a teacher before the expiration of the term for which such teacher was employed, the District Board of School Directors shall give the said teacher a written discharge signed by the President thereof, and countersigned by the Secretary, which discharge shall state fully the cause of said dismissal.

RULE 46.—The president of each board of district directors and the directors of each sub-district, shall be required to furnish each youth in their respective districts and sub-districts, entitled to admission to the public schools of the State, with a printed certificate designating the proper school at which the holder is entitled to attend, and no pupil shall be entitled to admission to any other school than the one to which they are assigned by said certificate, and no certificate shall be granted to any youth unless within the ages prescribed by law.

Rule 47.—The secretaries of the district boards of school directors will, in addition to the regular reports required of them by law, to their respective Division Superintendents, make, in connection therewith, full and complete reports of all school lands in their districts, the amount and condition of the same, and any changes that may occur therein by sale, rent, or otherwise, and shall make it their especial care to see that such lands are not trespassed upon, or in any way laid to waste, and will make such other reports as the said Division Superintendents may at any time direct.

Rule 48.—If, in any ward of any parish, an organization cannot be effected for school purposes, through lack of suitable persons to be appointed as school directors or otherwise, such ward shall be merged into the ward next most contiguous, forming one school district therewith; the superintendent of the division designating with what contiguous ward it shall be merged, and the Board of School Directors of the ward to which such unorganized district is joined, shall assume charge of the same, until such time as said ward can be satisfactorily organized.

Rule 49.—The District Boards of School Directors shall adopt the text books recommended by the State School Board.

Office State Board of Education,
New Orleans, Louisiana, September 14, 1869.

The foregoing Rules and Regulations were this day adopted by the State Board of Education by the following vote :

Ayes—Messrs. Jules A. Mathieu, V. E. McCarthy, E. W. Pierce, John Turner and J. R. West—5.

Nays—None.

J. R. WEST,
President pro tem. of the Board.

E. S. Stoddard,
Secretary of the Board.

www.ingramcontent.com/pod-product-compliance
Lightning Source LLC
Chambersburg PA
CBHW031448270326
41930CB00007B/913
9783337779498